COME
UNTO ME

Daily Scriptures and Quotes

COME UNTO ME

Daily Scriptures and Quotes

ED J. PINEGAR & RICHARD J. ALLEN

Covenant Communications, Inc.

Cover image *Christ Appears to the Nephites* © Gary Kapp
All interior images © Gary Kapp

Cover design copyrighted 2003 by Covenant Communications, Inc.

Published by Covenant Communications, Inc.
American Fork, Utah

Printed in Canada
First Printing: October 2003

09 08 07 06 05   10 9 8 7 6 5 4

ISBN 1-59156-278-3

Preface

This modest collection of inspirational quotes and scriptural references is intended to brighten your day, kindle the glow of spiritual awareness in your life, and stimulate prayerful consideration of many of the grand gospel themes that are aligned with "a godly walk and conversation" (D&C 20:69). Sayings from all the presidents of the Church in this dispensation—from Joseph Smith to Gordon B. Hinckley—are included here, together with a selection from the sermons and writings of many of the other Apostles and General Authorities. Each of the general presidents of the Relief Society, beginning with Emma Smith, is represented, plus a number of other noted auxiliary leaders.

We sincerely hope this anthology will serve as a daily uplift of spirit and testimony and a helpful source of wisdom for lessons, talks, leadership training, and family home evening sessions. May we all feast on the word of the Lord more often, gratefully listen to the counsel of our inspired leaders more willingly, and humbly seek to follow God's will with increased conviction and devotion. The object is to hear the voice of the Lord more surely in our lives each day—and to obey in faith and hope. "My word shall not pass away," declared the Lord, "but shall all be fulfilled, whether by mine own voice or by the voice of my servants, it is the same" (D&C 1:38).

Ed J. Pinegar
Richard J. Allen

JANUARY

Therefore I would that ye should be perfect even as I, or your Father who is in heaven is perfect.

—3 Nephi 12:48

JANUARY 1
Approaching Perfection

Therefore I would that ye should be perfect even as I, or your Father who is in heaven is perfect.

3 NE. 12:48

See also Matt. 5:48; D&C 93:11–14, 19–20.

We consider that God has created man with a mind capable of instruction, and a faculty which may be enlarged in proportion to the heed and diligence given to the light communicated from heaven to the intellect; and that the nearer man approaches perfection, the clearer are his views, and the greater his enjoyments, till he has overcome the evils of his life and lost every desire for sin; and like the ancients, arrives at that point of faith where he is wrapped in the power and glory of his Maker, and is caught up to dwell with Him.

(Joseph Smith, *History of The Church of Jesus Christ of Latter-day Saints*, 7 Vols., ed. B. H. Roberts [1932–1951], 2:8.)

JANUARY 2
Planning for the Future

And now, the plan of mercy could not be brought about except an atonement should be made; therefore God himself atoneth for the sins of the world, to bring about the plan of mercy, to appease the demands of justice, that God might be a perfect, just God, and a merciful God also.

ALMA 42:15

See also 2 Ne. 9:13; 11:5; Alma 34:9.

A prerequisite for "doing" is goal setting. Actions are preceded by thoughts and planning. All of us must take charge of our own lives. We must evaluate the choices that are open to us, and then we must act positively on our own decision. An old proverb states, "A journey of one thousand miles begins with the first step." The word straightway suggests the urgency to take that first step toward any worthy goal.

(Marvin J. Ashton, Be of Good Cheer [Salt Lake City: Deseret Book, 1987], 56–57.)

JANUARY 3

Organizing Your Day

Organize yourselves; prepare every needful thing; and establish a house, even a house of prayer, a house of fasting, a house of faith, a house of learning, a house of glory, a house of order, a house of God.

D&C 88:119

See also Matt. 6:33; Mosiah 4:27; D&C 88:124.

First, after you have determined your values and priorities, write them down into long–term and short–term goals. . . . Prioritize each goal. . . . [L]ist for each day three items that are both important and urgent.... Pray for guidance and direction on how to accomplish the tasks before you. . . . What should our priorities be? The Savior taught, "Seek ye first the kingdom of God, and his righteousness; and all these things shall be added unto you" (Matthew 6:33).

(Joseph B. Wirthlin, *Finding Peace in Our Lives* [Salt Lake City: Deseret Book, 1995], 224.)

JANUARY 4

Cultivating a Good Attitude

For as he thinketh in his heart, so is he.

PROV. 23:7

See also 1 John 3:3; Enos 1:9; Moro. 7:6–8.

I hope that we will cultivate an attitude of looking for positive elements that lead to growth and enthusiasm.

(Gordon B. Hinckley, Faith: The Essence of True Religion [Salt Lake City: Deseret Book, 1989], 77.)

JANUARY 5
Making Choices

And if it seem evil unto you to serve the Lord, choose you this day whom ye will serve; whether the gods which your fathers served that were on the other side of the flood, or the gods of the Amorites, in whose land ye dwell: but as for me and my house, we will serve the Lord.

JOSH. 24:15

See also 2 Ne. 2:27; 10:23; 17:16.

Our choice is to seek to establish His righteousness or to rebelliously continue to walk in our own way. We are free to choose, to obey or not to obey, to come to terms or not to come to terms with the Lord. But we cannot revise the terms.

(Neal A. Maxwell, *Notwithstanding My Weakness* [Salt Lake City: Deseret Book, 1981], 76.)

JANUARY 6

Forming Good Habits

O, remember, my son, and learn wisdom in thy youth; yea, learn in thy youth to keep the commandments of God.

ALMA 37:35

See also Mosiah 5:2; JS—H 1:28.

First, I would suggest that we teach youth by our own example the importance of acquiring good habits. Bad habits can be such fatal pitfalls. First we could break them if we would, then we would break them if we could. "Ill habits," said John Dryden, "gather by unseen degrees, as brooks make rivers, and rivers run to seas." Good habits, on the other hand, are the soul's muscles; the more you use them, the stronger they grow.

(Thomas S. Monson, *Be Your Best Self* [Salt Lake City: Deseret Book, 1979], 93.)

JANUARY 7

Overcoming Adversity

If thou be cast into the deep; if the billowing surge conspire against thee; if fierce winds become thine enemy; if the heavens gather blackness, and all the elements combine to hedge up the way; and above all, if the very jaws of hell shall gape open the mouth wide after thee, know thou, my son, that all these things shall give thee experience, and shall be for thy good.

D&C 122:7

See also 2 Ne. 2:11–12, 15; Alma 62:41; D&C 136:31.

Thus illuminated by the light of faith, adversity becomes a vehicle for growth, and death becomes a doorway from one phase of our eternal existence to another.

(M. Russell Ballard, *Our Search for Happiness: An Invitation to Understand The Church of Jesus Christ of Latter-day Saints* [Salt Lake City: Deseret Book, 1993], 78.)

JANUARY 8

Setting and Achieving Goals

Verily I say, men should be anxiously engaged in a good cause, and do many things of their own free will, and bring to pass much righteousness;

For the power is in them, wherein they are agents unto themselves. And inasmuch as men do good they shall in nowise lose their reward.

D&C 58:27–28

See also 3 Ne. 12:48; 27:27; D&C 88:119.

The Church sets standards for us in many areas, but many of the standards of personal performance must be set by us. An unwillingness to set standards or goals for ourselves, of course, can result in a Mormon malaise, going nowhere—but very anxiously. Setting and achieving goals can give us spiritual momentum in our lives and deserved self-esteem. This pattern of achievement is self-reinforcing and produces a contagion that affects others as well as ourselves.

(Neal A. Maxwell, *Deposition of a Disciple* [Salt Lake City: Deseret Book, 1976], 71–72.)

JANUARY 9

Repentance Fosters Forgiveness
and Blessings

Behold, he who has repented of his sins, the same is forgiven, and I, the Lord, remember them no more.

By this ye may know if a man repenteth of his sins—behold, he will confess them and forsake them.

D&C 58:42–43

See also Mosiah 27:24; 3 Ne. 23:5; D&C 42:28.

There is hope for all to be healed through repentance and obedience. The Prophet Isaiah verified that "though your sins be as scarlet, they shall be as white as snow" (Isaiah 1:18). The Prophet Joseph Smith stated: "There is never a time when the spirit is too old to approach God. All are [in] reach of pardoning mercy" (Joseph Smith, *Teachings of the Prophet Joseph Smith*, se. Joseph fielding Smith [1976], 191). After our full repentance, the formula is wonderfully simple. Indeed, the Lord has given it to us in these words: "Will ye not now return unto me, and repent of your sins, and be converted, that I may heal you?" (3 Ne. 9:13).

(James E. Faust, *Finding Light in a Dark World* [Salt Lake City: Deseret Book, 1995], 31.)

JANUARY 10

Making Perseverance a Part of Your Life

Therefore, my beloved brethren, be ye stedfast, unmoveable, always abounding in the work of the Lord, forasmuch as ye know that your labour is not in vain in the Lord.

1 COR. 15:58

See also 1 Ne. 1:21; 2 Ne. 31:20; Mosiah 5:15; Hel. 6:1.

"What prompts such devotion on the part of every worker?" The answer can be stated simply: an individual testimony of the gospel of the Lord Jesus Christ, even a heartfelt desire to love the Lord with all one's heart, mind, and soul, and one's neighbor as oneself.

(Thomas S. Monson, *Be Your Best Self* [Salt Lake City: Deseret Book, 1979], 181.)

JANUARY 11
Giving Selfless Service

And behold, I tell you these things that ye may learn wisdom; that ye may learn that when ye are in the service of your fellow beings ye are only in the service of your God.

MOSIAH 2:17

See also Matt. 16:15; Mosiah 4:15; D&C 4:2.

The followers of the divine Christ have to be weighed on the scales of what their actions are rather than on solemn professions of belief. The true measure is found in Matthew: "Inasmuch as ye have done it unto one of the least of these . . . ye have done it unto me" (Matthew 25:40). A wise man observed, "The man who lives by himself and for himself is apt to be corrupted by the company he keeps."

(James E. Faust, *To Reach Even unto You* [Salt Lake City: Deseret Book, 1980], 109.)

JANUARY 12
Keeping Commitments

For behold, this is my work and my glory—to
bring to pass the immortality and eternal life of man.

MOSES 1:39

See also D&C 18:6; 58:3; Morm. 5:14.

Commitment as a word cannot stand alone. We
must always ask, "Committed to what?" As all of us
blend into the programs of the Church, it behooves us
to set goals for ourselves in order to reap the blessings
of self-improvement and excellent performance in
given assignments.

(Marvin J. Ashton, *Be of Good Cheer* [Salt Lake City: Deseret
Book, 1987], 48.)

JANUARY 13
Progressing Eternally

And if thou art faithful unto the end thou shalt have a crown of immortality, and eternal life in the mansions which I have prepared in the house of my Father.

D&C 81:6

See also 2 Ne. 28:30; Alma 13:3; Abr. 3:25–26.

"As man now is, God once was; as God now is, man may be."

(Lorenzo Snow, *The Teachings of Lorenzo Snow*, ed. Clyde J. Williams [Salt Lake City: Bookcraft, 1984], viii.)

JANUARY 14

Showing Gratitude

Wherefore be ye not unwise, but understanding what the will of the Lord is. . . . Giving thanks always for all things unto God and the Father in the name of our Lord Jesus Christ.

EPH. 5:17, 20

See also Mosiah 2:20; Alma 34:38; D&C 59:21.

The grateful man sees our society as afflicted by a spirit of thoughtless arrogance unbecoming those who have been so magnificently blessed. How grateful we should be for the bounties we enjoy. Absence of gratitude is the mark of the narrow, uneducated mind. It bespeaks a lack of knowledge and the ignorance of self-sufficiency. It expresses itself in ugly egotism and frequently in wanton mischief. . . . Where there is appreciation, there is courtesy, there is concern for the rights and property of others. Without appreciation, there is arrogance and evil.

(Gordon B. Hinckley, *Teachings of Gordon B. Hinckley* [Salt Lake City: Deseret Book, 1997], 247.)

JANUARY 15
Learning the Things of Life

Angels speak by the power of the Holy Ghost; wherefore, they speak the words of Christ. Wherefore, I said unto you, feast upon the words of Christ; for behold, the words of Christ will tell you all things what ye should do.

2 NE. 32:3

See also D&C 68:4; 105:1.

We can learn how to think, how to plan, how to organize, how to worship, and how to work. We have the holy books of scripture through which we may learn about God himself and become familiar with his great doctrines, his standards of value, and his will concerning us.

(Howard W. Hunter, *The Teachings of Howard W. Hunter*, ed. Clyde J. Williams [Salt Lake City: Bookcraft, 1997], 178.)

JANUARY 16
Following the Will of God

Blessed art thou, Nephi, for those things which thou hast done; for I have beheld how thou hast with unwearyingness declared the word, which I have given unto thee, unto this people. And thou hast not feared them, and hast not sought thine own life, but hast sought my will, and to keep my commandments.

HEL. 10:4

See also Mark 3:35; John 7:17; D&C 46:30.

Another cosmic fact: only by aligning our wills with God's is full happiness to be found. Anything less results in a lesser portion (see Alma 12:10–11). The Lord will work with us even if, at first, we "can no more than desire" but are willing to "give place for a portion of [His] words" (Alma 32:27). A small foothold is all He needs. But we must desire and provide it.

(Neal A. Maxwell, *If Thou Endure It Well* [Salt Lake City: Bookcraft, 1996], 51.)

JANUARY 17
Seeking Unity of Purpose

Behold, this I have given unto you as a parable, and it is even as I am. I say unto you, be one; and if ye are not one ye are not mine.

D&C 38:27

See also 2 Cor. 13:11; 1 Pet. 3:8; D&C 35:2.

Unity of purpose, thought, and feeling are exalting qualities. When we can put aside our differences and value each others' strengths, great things happen. The Prophet Joseph Smith admonished, "Don't be limited in your views with regard to your neighbor's virtue. . . . You must enlarge your souls towards each other." Such generosity of spirit invites greater unity.

(Mary Ellen Smoot, "Developing Inner Strength," *Ensign*, May 2002, 14.)

JANUARY 18
Avoiding Pride

Behold, I speak unto you, Oliver, a few words. Behold, thou art blessed, and art under no condemnation. But beware of pride, lest thou shouldst enter into temptation.

D&C 23:1

See also Matt. 23:12; 1 Tim. 3:6; 1 Ne. 11:36.

Pride is a sin that can readily be seen in others but is rarely admitted in ourselves. Most of us consider pride to be a sin of those on the top, such as the rich and the learned, looking down at the rest of us. (See 2 Ne. 9:42.) There is, however, a far more common ailment among us—and that is pride from the bottom looking up. It is manifest in so many ways, such as faultfinding, gossiping, backbiting, murmuring, living beyond our means, envying, coveting, withholding gratitude and praise that might lift another, and being unforgiving and jealous.

(Ezra Taft Benson, "Beware of Pride," *Ensign*, May 1989, 5–6.)

JANUARY 19

Desiring Good

And it is requisite with the justice of God that men should be judged according to their works; and if their works were good in this life, and the desires of their hearts were good, that they should also, at the last day, be restored unto that which is good.

ALMA 41:3

See also Mosiah 18:10, 12; Moro. 7:9; 10:4.

In the great plan of salvation nothing has been overlooked. The gospel of Jesus Christ is the most beautiful thing in the world. It embraces every soul whose heart is right and who diligently seeks him and desires to obey his laws and covenants. Therefore, if a person is for any cause denied the privilege of complying with any of the covenants, the Lord will judge him or her by the intent of the heart.

(Dallin H. Oaks, *Pure in Heart* [Salt Lake City: Bookcraft, 1988], 62.)

Verily I say unto you all: Arise and shine forth, that thy light may be a standard for the nations.

D&C 115:5

See also Alma 46:36; 62:4–5.

Martin Luther King once said, "The ultimate measure of a man is not where he stands in moments of comfort and convenience, but where he stands at times of challenge and controversy. The true neighbor will risk his position, his prestige, and even his life for the welfare of others. In dangerous valleys and hazardous pathways, he will lift some bruised and beaten brother to a higher and more noble life."

(Martin Luther King, Jr., *Strength to Love* [New York: Harper and Row, 1963].)

JANUARY 21

Promises for the Obedient

If ye keep my commandments, ye shall abide in my love; even as I have kept my Father's commandments, and abide in his love.

JOHN 15:10

See also 1 Sam. 15:22; John 14:15; Heb. 5:8.

The satisfying thing is that obedience brings happiness; it brings peace; it brings growth—all of these to the individual, and his good example brings respect for the institution of which he is a part.

(Gordon B. Hinckley, *Be Thou an Example* [Salt Lake City: Deseret Book, 1981], 12.)

JANUARY 22

Becoming Converted to Jesus Christ

Even so ye must be born again into the kingdom of heaven, of water, and of the Spirit, and be cleansed by blood, even the blood of mine Only Begotten; that ye might be sanctified from all sin, and enjoy the words of eternal life in this world, and eternal life in the world to come, even immortal glory.

MOSES 6:59

See also Mosiah 5:2, 7; Moro. 8:25–26.

But all that has happened in the past has not, and all that occurs in the future will not change the truth that conversion to Jesus Christ and his gospel is the one and only way; for still it must be said that "there is none other way given under heaven by which men must be saved." (See Acts 4:12.)

(Elder Marion G. Romney, *Conference Report*, October 1963, Afternoon Meeting, 26.)

JANUARY 23
Do Your Whole Duty

Let us hear the conclusion of the whole matter: Fear God, and keep his commandments: for this is the whole duty of man.

Eccl. 12:13

See also Moro. 9:6; D&C 107:99–100.

If I do my duty, according to my understanding of the requirements that the Lord has made of me, then I ought to have a conscience void of offense; I ought to have satisfaction in my soul, in the consciousness that I have simply done my duty as I understand it, and I will risk the consequences. With me it is a matter between me and the Lord; so it is with every one of us.

(Joseph F. Smith, Gospel Doctrine: Selections from the *Sermons and Writings of Joseph F. Smith*, comp. John A. Widtsoe [Salt Lake City: Deseret Book, 1939], 249.)

JANUARY 24

Serving as a Leader

But he that is greatest among you shall be your servant.

MATT. 23:11

See also John 13:15; Jarom 1:7.

A love of people is essential to effective leadership. Do you love those whom you work with? Do you realize the worth of souls is great in the sight of God (see D&C 18:10)? Do you have faith in youth? Do you find yourself praising their virtues, commending them for their accomplishments? Or do you have a critical attitude toward them because of their mistakes?

(Ezra Taft Benson, "Leadership and the Needs of Youth," *Improvement Era,* Aug. 1948, 494.)

JANUARY 25

Having Hope in Christ

For, for this intent have we written these things, that they may know that we knew of Christ, and we had a hope of his glory many hundred years before his coming; and not only we ourselves had a hope of his glory, but also all the holy prophets which were before us.

JACOB 4:4

See also 2 Thes. 2:13; Titus 2:16; Moro. 7:41.

We were not left without hope. Our Savior, through his atonement, has made it possible for us to obtain salvation. He will not leave us helpless as we struggle to overcome the adversities of this life.

(Barbara W. Winder, "Hope in Christ," *Ensign,* Nov. 1986, 90.)

JANUARY 26

Seeking Wisdom

And as all have not faith, seek ye diligently and teach one another words of wisdom; yea, seek ye out of the best books words of wisdom; seek learning, even by study and also by faith.

D&C 88:118

See also Prov. 2:6; Matt. 7:24; 1 Cor. 3:19.

That wisdom which leads to salvation comes from God by revelation. Every person on earth, in or out of the Church, can gain wisdom from the Lord, who is the source and font of all truth and righteousness.

(Bruce R. McConkie, *Doctrinal New Testament Commentary*, 3 vols. [Salt Lake City: Bookcraft, 1966–73], 3:246.)

JANUARY 27
Developing a Christlike Character

We believe in being honest, true, chaste, benevolent, virtuous, and in doing good to all men.

A OF F 1:13

See also 3 Ne. 12:48; 27:27.

And what is the crowning glory of man in this earth so far as his individual achievement is concerned? It is *character—character developed through obedience to the laws of life as revealed through the gospel of Jesus Christ, who came that we might have life and have it more abundantly.* Man's chief concern in life should not be the acquiring of gold nor fame nor material possessions. It should *not* be the development of physical prowess nor of intellectual strength, *but his aim, the highest in life, should be the development of a Christlike character.*

(David O. McKay, *Man May Know for Himself: Teachings of President David O. McKay,* comp. Clare Middlemiss [Salt Lake City: Deseret Book, 1967], 29.)

JANUARY 28

Beware of Hypocrisy

Thou hypocrite, first cast the beam out of thine own eye; and then shalt thou see clearly to cast the mote out of thy brother's eye.

3 NE. 14:5

See also 2 Ne. 31:13; 3 Ne. 13:5; D&C 121:37.

It has seemed to me that the one sin that the Savior condemned as much as any other was the sin of hypocrisy—the living of the double life, the life we let our friends and sometimes our wives believe, and the life we actually live.

(J. Reuben Clark Jr., *Behold the Lamb of God* [Salt Lake City: Deseret Book, 1991], 294.)

And the Spirit shall be given unto you by the prayer of faith; and if ye receive not the Spirit ye shall not teach.

D&C 42:14

See also Mosiah 23:14; Alma 17:2–3; D&C 28.

In my opinion no greater call can come to anyone than to be a teacher in The Church of Jesus Christ of Latter-day Saints. We are all teachers in one way or another, whether we have been called and set apart as such or not. The Savior himself was known as the greatest of all teachers. Let us try in every way to emulate him and his example.

(N. Eldon Tanner, "Teaching Children of God," *Ensign,* Oct. 1980, 2.)

JANUARY 30
Purifying the Heart

And I give unto you, who are the first laborers in this last kingdom, a commandment that you assemble yourselves together, and organize yourselves, and prepare yourselves, and sanctify yourselves; yea, purify your hearts, and cleanse your hands and your feet before me, that I may make you clean.

D&C 88:74

See also 1 Pet. 1:22; Hel. 3:35; 3 Ne. 19:28.

To be "pure in heart" is to achieve that condition in which motives, desires, and attitudes are acceptable to God and consistent with the eternal progress that is the ultimate destiny of his children.

(Dallin H. Oaks, *Pure in Heart* [Salt Lake City: Bookcraft, 1988], 137.)

JANUARY 31

"Feed My Sheep"

Let the residue of the elders watch over the churches, and declare the word in the regions round about them; and let them labor with their own hands that there be no idolatry nor wickedness practised.

D&C 52:39

See also 1 Ne. 22:24; Alma 5:37–40.

The members of the Church are the sheep. They are His, and we are called by Him to watch over them. We are to do more than warn them against danger. We are to feed them.

(Henry B. Eyring, "Watch with Me," *Ensign*, May 2001, 38.)

EBRUARY

*Seek ye first the Kingdom of God
and his righteousness . . .*

—3 Nephi 13:33

FEBRUARY 1

A Willing Sacrifice

And ye shall offer for a sacrifice unto me a broken heart and a contrite spirit. And whoso cometh unto me with a broken heart and a contrite spirit, him will I baptize with fire and with the Holy Ghost, even as the Lamanites, because of their faith in me at the time of their conversion, were baptized with fire and with the Holy Ghost, and they knew it not.

3 NE. 9:20

See also 2 Ne. 2:7; Omni 1:26; 3 Ne. 24:3.

Christ's example of obedience and sacrifice becomes ours. How grateful we should be for the word of God and that we can choose to hear it and obey. We are privileged to offer sacrifice by making sacred the thoughts and deeds of our lives so that they might be more like his. In so doing, the blessings of heaven may be ours now and forever.

(Russell M. Nelson, *The Power within Us* [Salt Lake City: Deseret Book, 1988], 57.)

FEBRUARY 2
Accessing the Quiet Miracle

And now it came to pass that according to our record, and we know our record to be true, for behold, it was a just man who did keep the record—for he truly did many miracles in the name of Jesus; and there was not any man who could do a miracle in the name of Jesus save he were cleansed every whit from his iniquity.

3 NE. 8:1

See also Mark 9:39; 1 Cor. 12:29; 3 Ne. 1:4.

How do we access the quiet miracle that the Lord works as He transforms us, His children, into worthy heirs of the kingdom of God? I believe it is made possible because "God so loved the world, that he gave his only begotten Son, that whosoever believeth in him should not perish, but have everlasting life" (John 3:16). I believe it comes as we yield to the enticings of the Spirit, put off the natural man, and are filled with the love of God (see Mosiah 3:19).

(Sydney S. Reynolds, "A God of Miracles," *Ensign*, May 2001, 12.)

FEBRUARY 3

Seek Counsel from the Lord

Wherefore, brethren, seek not to counsel the Lord, but to take counsel from his hand. For behold, ye yourselves know that he counseleth in wisdom, and in justice, and in great mercy, over all his works.

JACOB 4:10

See also 1 Cor. 2:11–16; 2 Ne. 9:28–29.

When we strive to be Christlike, he is "formed" in us; if we open the door, he will enter; if we seek his counsel, he will counsel us.

(Howard W. Hunter, *The Teachings of Howard W. Hunter*, ed. Clyde J. Williams [Salt Lake City: Bookcraft, 1997], 33.)

FEBRUARY 4
Be an Example

For I have given you an example, that ye should do as I have done to you.

JOHN 13:15

See also 2 Ne. 31:9; Jacob 2:35; Alma 39:11.

Behold your little ones and teach them. I need not remind you that your example will do more than anything else in impressing upon their minds a pattern of life. It is always interesting to meet the children of old friends and to find in another generation the ways of their fathers and mothers.

(Gordon B. Hinckley, *Be Thou an Example* [Salt Lake City: Deseret Book, 1981], 38.)

FEBRUARY 5

Conquering Procrastination

For behold, this life is the time for men to prepare to meet God; yea, behold the day of this life is the day for men to perform their labors.

And now, as I said unto you before, as ye have had so many witnesses, therefore, I beseech of you that ye do not procrastinate the day of your repentance until the end; for after this day of life, which is given us to prepare for eternity, behold, if we do not improve our time while in this life, then cometh the night of darkness wherein there can be no labor performed.

ALMA 34:32–33

See also Joshua 24:15; Luke 12:47; Alma 13:27.

The foolish virgins were not averse to buying oil. They knew they should have oil. They merely procrastinated, not knowing when the bridegroom would come. . . . Midnight is so late for those who have procrastinated.

(Spencer W. Kimball, *Faith Precedes the Miracle* [Salt Lake City: Deseret Book, 1972], 255.)

FEBRUARY 6
Cooperation: A Principle of Power

Can two walk together, except they be agreed?

AMOS 3:3

See also John 17:4; D&C 38:27; 107:27.

Cooperation is a principle of tremendous power. One man may be weak; but a thousand, standing together, are strong. One man may stand helpless before the fallen tree; but the many will carry it away easily. One man may shout a truth with little avail; but a thousand voices will be heard by the multitude.

(John A. Widtsoe, *An Understandable Religion* [Independence, Mo.: Zion's Printing and Publishing Co., 1944], 180.)

FEBRUARY 7
How Should We Judge?

And now it came to pass that when Jesus had spoken these words he turned again to the multitude, and did open his mouth unto them again, saying: Verily, verily, I say unto you, Judge not, that ye be not judged.

3 NE. 14:1

See also Luke 6:37–38, 41–42; JST, Matt. 7:1–8.

Man is prone to entertain wrong thoughts of his neighbor and to pass judgment upon his fellows, little realizing that to judge righteously requires the wisdom of divinity. The world will be happier and more Christlike only as it cherishes right thinking and makes applicable in social life and particularly in religious circles the injunction of the Savior.

(David O. McKay, *Pathways to Happiness* [Salt Lake City: Bookcraft, 1957], 322.)

FEBRUARY 8
Courageous Leadership

Be strong and of a good courage, fear not, nor be afraid . . . for the Lord thy God, he it is that doth go with thee; he will not fail thee, nor forsake thee.

DEUT. 31:6

See also Ps. 31:24; Alma 56:45.

Leaders must be courageous. One of the highest qualities of all true leadership is a high standard of courage. When we speak of courage and leadership we are using terms that stand for the quality of life by which men determine consciously the proper course to pursue and stand with fidelity to their convictions.

(Boyd K. Packer, *The Holy Temple* [Salt Lake City: Bookcraft, 1980], 179.)

FEBRUARY 9

Partaking of the Sacrament

O God, the Eternal Father, we ask thee in the name of thy Son, Jesus Christ, to bless and sanctify this bread to the souls of all those who partake of it; that they may eat in remembrance of the body of thy Son, and witness unto thee, O God, the Eternal Father, that they are willing to take upon them the name of thy Son, and always remember him, and keep his commandments which he hath given them, that they may always have his Spirit to be with them. Amen.

MORO. 4:3

See also Matt. 26:26–28; 3 Nephi:12–13.

Our personal reward for compliance with the covenants and obligations in the ordinance of the sacrament is companionship of God's Holy Spirit. This is the light that leads to eternal life. The divine virtues associated with the partaking of the Lord's Supper are (1) keeping his divine life ever in mind; (2) loving him with all our heart, might, mind, and strength; and (3) laboring to bring to pass his ultimate purpose—the eternal life of man.

(David B. Haight, *A Light unto the World* [Salt Lake City: Deseret Book, 1997], 176–177.)

FEBRUARY 10
Balancing Our Lives

And see that all these things are done in wisdom and order; for it is not requisite that a man should run faster than he has strength. And again, it is expedient that he should be diligent, that thereby he might win the prize; therefore, all things must be done in order.

MOSIAH 4:27

See also 2 Tim. 3:1–4.

As we pursue our careers and develop our purposes, we need to keep in mind the broader objectives of our time on earth, to achieve a balance and richness in our personal lives.

(Thomas S. Monson, *Pathways to Perfection* [Salt Lake City: Deseret Book, 1973], 108.)

FEBRUARY 11
Blessed are the Peacemakers

And blessed are all the peacemakers, for they shall be called the children of God.

3 NE. 12:9

See also Matt. 5:9; Rom. 10:15; Mosiah 29:14.

Now, if you don't want to quarrel, take measures to prevent it. That is what we are after. We are trying to get the people to hearken to counsel that will prevent a quarrel, and a serious one. If you can prevent a quarrel in a family you do a good thing. "Blessed are the peacemakers." We are peacemakers. We are preserving the peace.

(Brigham Young, *Journal of Discourses*, 26 vols. [London: Latter-day Saints' Book Depot, 1854–1886], 12: 316.)

FEBRUARY 12
Building a Community of Saints

Therefore, strengthen your brethren in all your conversation, in all your prayers, in all your exhortations, and in all your doings.

D&C 108:7

See also Matt. 6:33; 25:40; D&C 50:26.

In any community of Saints, we all work to serve each other in the best way we know how. Our work has a higher purpose because it is work to bless others and to build the kingdom of God.

(L. Tom Perry, "Building a Community of Saints," *Ensign*, May 2001, 35.)

FEBRUARY 13
Compassion for All

Thus speaketh the Lord of hosts, saying, Execute true judgment, and shew mercy and compassions every man to his brother.

ZECH. 7:9

See also Matt. 18:33; Luke 10:33; 1 Pet. 3:8.

The Saints are to have love and compassion for everyone. God grant that we may so live and let our light so shine that others, seeing our good works, will be constrained to glorify his name. Let there be in our hearts love and compassion and consideration and charity for every soul that we come in contact with.

(George Albert Smith, *The Teachings of George Albert* Smith, ed. Robert McIntosh and Susan McIntosh [Salt Lake City: Bookcraft, 1996], 135.)

FEBRUARY 14

Enhancing Our Temple Experience

And that thou mayest more fully keep thyself unspotted from the world, thou shalt go to the house of prayer and offer up thy sacraments upon my holy day.

D&C 59:9

See also Hel. 4:24; D&C 88:119; 109:8.

There is a difference in just attending the temple and having a rich spiritual experience. The real blessings of the temple come as we enhance our temple experience. To do so, we must feel a spirit of reverence for the temple and a spirit of worship.

(L. Lionel Kendrick, "Enhancing Our Temple Experience," *Ensign*, May 2001, 78.)

FEBRUARY 15
The Victory of Self-Control

And every man that striveth for the mastery is temperate in all things. Now they do it to obtain a corruptible crown; but we an incorruptible.

1 COR. 9:25

See also James 4:7; 1 Pet. 3:10; Alma 37:32–35.

I consider one of the greatest victories for a man to gain is to learn how to control himself. Show me a man that does control himself and I will show you a safe man; or a man that has prepared himself by this principle is on the road to salvation. A man that is prepared to lay all that he hath upon the altar, and his life with it, for the Gospel's sake and the kingdom of God, is in the right way, but the moment that we teach a doctrine that we do not practice we show our weakness.

(Wilford Woodruff, *Journal of Discourses*, 26 vols. [London: Latter-day Saints' Book Depot, 1854–1886], 4:98.)

FEBRUARY 16

*Happiness Is the Object and Design
of Our Existence*

He that handleth a matter wisely shall find good:
and whoso trusteth in the Lord, happy is he.

Prov. 16:20

See also Prov. 29:18; John 13:17; 1 Pet. 3:14.

Happiness is the object and design of our
existence; and will be the end thereof, if we pursue
the path that leads to it; and this path is virtue,
uprightness, faithfulness, holiness, and keeping all
the commandments of God.

(Joseph Smith, *Teachings of the Prophet Joseph Smith*, sel.
Joseph Fielding Smith [1976], 255–56.)

FEBRUARY 17
Helping Others Build Faith

And the apostles said unto the Lord, Increase our faith.

See also Rom. 10:17; Gal. 3:11; Heb.11:1.

Rather, let us go forward with faith and with the vision of the great and marvelous future that lies ahead as this work grows in strength and gains in momentum. Build faith in the hearts of all those around you.

(Gordon B. Hinckley "Go Forward with Faith," *Ensign*, August 1986, 5.)

FEBRUARY 18
Finding Inner Strength

The Lord is my strength and song, and he is become my salvation: he is my God, and I will prepare him an habitation; my father's God, and I will exalt him.

Ex. 15:2

See also Ps. 71:16; Alma 26:12; Ether 12:27.

What inner strength would be in every person if he knew that the Master and His teachings were indeed his great source of guidance, his great source of correct example, his great source of help! That is our prime goal in all our teaching in the home.

(Spencer W. Kimball, "Therefore I Was Taught," *Ensign*, Jan. 1982, 4.)

FEBRUARY 19
Agency: A Blessing and Challenge

And it is given unto them to know good from evil; wherefore they are agents unto themselves, and I have given unto you another law and commandment.
MOSES 6:56

See also D&C 101:78; Moses 4:3; 6:33.

Agency is the power to think, choose, and act for ourselves. It comes with endless opportunities, accompanied by responsibility and consequences. It is a blessing and a burden. Using this gift of agency wisely is critical today because never in the world's history have God's children been so blessed or so blatantly confronted with so many choices.

(Sharon G. Larsen, "Agency—A Blessing and a Burden," *Ensign*, Nov. 1999, 11.)

FEBRUARY 20
Spending Less Than We Receive

And behold, I am also a man of no small reputation among all those who know me; yea, and behold, I have many kindreds and friends, and I have also acquired much riches by the hand of my industry.

ALMA 10:4

See also Matt. 25:14–30; Mosiah 23:5.

If we are to be self-reliant and in a position to share, obviously we must acquire some resources. If we live within our means and avoid debt, resources can be accumulated. There are those with average incomes who, over a lifetime, do amass some means, and there are those who receive large salaries who do not. What is the difference? It is simply spending less than they receive, saving along the way, and taking advantage of the power of compound interest.

(Joe J. Christensen, "Greed, Selfishness, and Overindulgence," *Ensign*, May 1999, 9.)

FEBRUARY 21
Act on Our Opportunities

And see that ye have faith, hope, and charity, and then ye will always abound in good works.

ALMA 7:24

See also Alma 34:28; Morm. 9:29; D&C 6:13.

All of us face challenges in our daily lives. Yet in challenges lie some of our greatest opportunities. As we recognize and act on our opportunities, progress, happiness, and spiritual growth follow. We need to be involved in moving the Lord's work forward. . . . The opportunities available to us are endless.

(H. David Burton, "A Season of Opportunity," *Ensign*, Nov. 1998, 9.)

FEBRUARY 22
Keeping an Eternal Perspective

Give me understanding, and I shall keep thy law;
yea, I shall observe it with my whole heart.

Ps. 119:34

See also Prov. 17:27; Alma 32:28; D&C 76:12.

I know that this truth is a key to conversion,
retention, and activation. If we can help people first
understand the plan, they will find a deeper and
more permanent motivation to keep the commandments. . . . When we understand the great plan of
happiness, we are gaining an eternal perspective, and
the commandments, ordinances, covenants, and the
experiences, trials, and tribulations can be seen in
their true and eternal light.

(Jay E. Jensen, "Keep an Eternal Perspective," *Ensign*, May
2000, 27.)

FEBRUARY 23

Increasing the Light of the Savior in Our Lives

Therefore, gird up your loins, that you may be the children of light, and that day shall not overtake you as a thief.

D&C 106:5

See also Mosiah 5:7–9; D&C 50:23–25; 90:24.

Christ's light and the gospel message of light and salvation can be darkened in our own lives only by our disobedience and lack of faith. In like manner the Savior's light *increases* in our lives as we keep the commandments and strive continually to be like Him. For "that which is of God is light; and he that receiveth light, and continueth in God, receiveth more light; and that light groweth brighter and brighter" (D&C 50:24).

(Virginia U. Jensen, "Lead, Kindly Light," *Ensign*, Nov. 2000, 62.)

FEBRUARY 24
Let Your Light Shine

Verily, verily, I say unto you, I give unto you to be the light of this people. A city that is set on a hill cannot be hid.

3 NE. 12:14

See also 3 Ne. 12:13–16; 18:24; 25:12.

Let your light shine. When we put our hands upon the head of an individual to set him apart for any position—teaching position or position of leadership—we are lighting another candle in the household of God.

(Harold B. Lee, *The Teachings of Harold B. Lee*, ed. Clyde J. Williams [Salt Lake City: Bookcraft, 1996], 616.)

FEBRUARY 25
Observance of the Sabbath

And he commanded them that they should observe the sabbath day, and keep it holy, and also every day they should give thanks to the Lord their God.

MOSIAH 18:23

See also Ex. 20:12; Mark 2:27; D&C 59:9.

Our observance or nonobservance of the Sabbath is an unerring measure of our attitude toward the Lord personally and toward his suffering in Gethsemane, his death on the cross, and his resurrection from the dead. It is a sign of whether we are Christians in very deed, or whether our conversion is so shallow that commemoration of his atoning sacrifice means little or nothing to us.

(Mark E. Petersen, "The Sabbath Day," *Ensign*, May 1975, 49.)

FEBRUARY 26
Love Begets Love

But behold I say unto you, love your enemies, bless them that curse you, do good to them that hate you, and pray for them who despitefully use you and persecute you.

3 NE. 12:44

See also John 13:34–35; 1 Jn. 4:7–11; Moro. 8:26.

It is a time-honored adage that love begets love. Let us pour forth love—show forth everlasting increase; cast our bread upon the waters and we shall receive it after many days, increased to a hundredfold.

(Joseph Smith, *Teachings of the Prophet Joseph Smith*, sel. Joseph Fielding Smith [Salt Lake City: Deseret Book, 1976, 316.])

FEBRUARY 27

Know ye not that ye are the temple of God, and that the Spirit of God dwelleth in you?

If any man defile the temple of God, him shall God destroy; for the temple of God is holy, which temple ye are.

1 Cor. 3:16–17

See also D&C 89.

Health is one of the most precious gifts of God to man. All the wealth in the world cannot produce health. Sick people, of course, are sometimes benefited by medicine. But sickness and disease for the most part come upon us by our disregard for the commandments of God.

(Heber J. Grant, *Gospel Standards: Selections from the Sermons and Writings of Heber J. Grant*, comp. G. Homer Durham [Salt Lake City: Improvement Era, 1981], 48.)

FEBRUARY 28

"Men Are, That They Might Have Joy"

Adam fell that men might be; and men are, that they might have joy.

2 NE. 2:25

See also 2 Ne. 2:23; Mosiah 2:41; 3 Ne. 27:31.

Sadness, disappointment, and severe challenge are *events* in life, not life itself. I do not minimize how hard some of these events are. They can extend over a long period of time, but they should not be allowed to become the confining center of everything you do. The Lord inspired Lehi to declare the fundamental truth, "Men are, that they might have joy."

(Richard G. Scott, "Finding Joy in Life," *Ensign*, May 1996, 24.)

FEBRUARY 29
Personal Liberty

And now remember, remember, my brethren, that whosoever perisheth, perisheth unto himself; and whosoever doeth iniquity, doeth it unto himself; for behold, ye are free; ye are permitted to act for yourselves; for behold, God hath given unto you a knowledge and he hath made you free.

HEL. 14:30

See also 2 Ne. 2:27; Alma 12:31; 13:3.

Free agency is the impelling source of the soul's progress. It is the purpose of the Lord that man become like him. In order for man to achieve this it was necessary for the Creator first to make him free. "Personal liberty," says Bulwer–Lytton, "is the paramount essential to human dignity and human happiness."

(David O. McKay, in Conference Report, Apr. 1950, 32–33.)

ARCH

The holy Spirit of God did enter into their hearts.

—HELAMAN 5:45

MARCH 1
Pray to Know the Book of Mormon Is True

And when ye shall receive these things, I would exhort you that ye would ask God, the Eternal Father, in the name of Christ, if these things are not true; and if ye shall ask with a sincere heart, with real intent, having faith in Christ, he will manifest the truth of it unto you, by the power of the Holy Ghost.

MORO. 10:4

See also 2 Ne. 25:18; 33:10–11; D&C 20:8–12.

You will find that when Moroni's promise is fulfilled and you are given the knowledge that the Book of Mormon is truly the word of God, there will come with it a witness that Jesus is the Christ, the Redeemer and Savior of the world. I have never known an instance where this did not occur.

(L. Aldin Porter, "To Bear Testimony of Mine Only Begotten," *Ensign*, May 2001, 30.)

MARCH 2
An Eternal Family

And in order to obtain the highest, a man must enter into this order of the priesthood [meaning the new and everlasting covenant of marriage].

D&C 131:2

See also D&C 132:4, 19; 136:4.

An eternal family begins when a young couple kneels at an altar in the holy temple of God and make covenants with each other and with God and receive His greatest promises. This sealing is preceded by each making and receiving covenants which, if they continue worthy, will bless them in this life as well as in the life to come.

(James E. Faust, "Eternity Lies before Us," *Ensign*, May 1997, 18.)

MARCH 3

Questions of Conscience for Parents

Provoke not your children to wrath: but bring them up in the nurture and admonition of the Lord.

EPH. 6:4

See also Jacob 3:10; Mosiah 1:4; 3 Ne. 18:21.

I have asked myself these questions: Do I leave my children exposed to danger when I don't teach them the truths of the gospel? Do I neglect their souls when I don't help them recognize the promptings of the Spirit and the guidance they can receive? Do I leave my children exposed to danger when my example is not the same as my words or when I don't share my love in such a way that each child feels it deeply?

(Patricia P. Pinegar, "Caring for the Souls of Children," *Ensign*, May 1997, 13–14.)

MARCH 4
The Right Kind of Success

And see that ye have faith, hope, and charity, and then ye will always abound in good works.

ALMA 7:24

See also Mosiah 2:41; Alma 29:14; D&C 15:6.

Ambition must be properly directed if we are to find true success. A man must have the ambition to succeed if he is to keep faith with himself, but ambition must be properly directed, not associated with evil, and the motivation must come from a worthy purpose. Joy and happiness in life are promised to those who have the right kind of success. We know that eternal joy is the purpose of man's creation, for the Lord said: "Men are, that they might have joy" (2 Ne. 2:25).

(Howard W. Hunter, *The Teachings of Howard W. Hunter*, ed. Clyde J. Williams [Salt Lake City: Bookcraft, 1997], 256.)

MARCH 5

Repenting of Our Selfishness

But behold, it is to get gain, to be praised of men, yea, and that ye might get gold and silver. And ye have set your hearts upon the riches and the vain things of this world, for the which ye do murder, and plunder, and steal, and bear false witness against your neighbor, and do all manner of iniquity.

HEL. 7:21

See also Isa. 56:11; Acts 5:3; D&C 56:8.

Selfishness is actually the detonator of all the cardinal sins. It is the hammer for the breaking of the Ten Commandments, whether by neglecting parents, the Sabbath, or by inducing false witness, murder, and envy. No wonder the selfish individual is often willing to break a covenant in order to fix an appetite. No wonder those who will later comprise the telestial kingdom, after they have paid a price, were once unrepentant adulterers, whoremongers, and those who both loved and made lies.

(Neal A. Maxwell, "Repent of Selfishness," *Ensign*, May 1999, 23.)

MARCH 6
Living by Faith

And Christ hath said: If ye will have faith in me ye shall have power to do whatsoever thing is expedient in me.

MORO. 7:33

See also 1 Ne. 16:28; 2 Ne. 26:13; Alma 14:26.

First, we should plant and nurture the seed of faith in the Lord Jesus Christ, our Savior and Redeemer. We each should develop the faith of Nephi to do the things the Lord has commanded (see 1 Nephi 3:7), knowing that all commandments are given for our good. . . . When the Lord instructed Nephi to build a ship, his brothers called him a fool to think he could do it. He told them: "If God had commanded me to do all things I could do them" (1 Nephi 17:50).

(Joseph B. Wirthlin, *Finding Peace in Our Lives* [Salt Lake City: Deseret Book, 1995], 215.)

MARCH 7
Make the Most of Each Day

And it shall come to pass that those that die in me shall not taste of death, for it shall be sweet unto them.
D&C 42:46

See also Alma 12:24; 43:32; D&C 45:2.

How fragile life, how certain death. We do not know when we will be required to leave this mortal existence. And so I ask, "What are we doing with today?" . . . . "I've been thinking about making some course corrections in my life. I plan to take the first step—tomorrow" . . . Because life is fragile and death inevitable, we must make the most of each day.

(President Thomas S. Monson, "Now Is the Time," *Ensign*, Nov. 2001, 60–61.)

MARCH 8
We Need Assistance

But the Comforter, which *is* the Holy Ghost, whom the Father will send in my name, he shall teach you all things, and bring all things to your remembrance, whatsoever I have said unto you.

JOHN 14:26

See also 1 Ne. 4:6; 2 Ne. 32:5; Moro. 8:26.

We need assistance. We are liable to do that which will lead us into trouble and darkness, and those things which will not tend to our good; but with the assistance of that Comforter which the Lord has promised His Saints, if we are careful to listen to its whisperings, and understand the nature of its language, we may avoid much trouble and serious difficulty.

(Lorenzo Snow, *The Teachings of Lorenzo Snow*, ed. Clyde J. Williams [Salt Lake City: Bookcraft, 1984], 108.)

MARCH 9
Tolerance Is Love

And now I would that ye should be humble, and be submissive and gentle; easy to be entreated; full of patience and long-suffering; being temperate in all things; being diligent in keeping the commandments of God at all times; asking for whatsoever things ye stand in need, both spiritual and temporal; always returning thanks unto God for whatsoever things ye do receive.

ALMA 7:23

See also Rom. 2:4; 3:25; Eph. 4:2.

A priesthood holder who is patient will be tolerant of the mistakes and failings of his loved ones. Because he loves them, he will not find fault nor criticize nor blame.

(Ezra Taft Benson, *The Teachings of Ezra Taft Benson* [Salt Lake City: Bookcraft, 1988], 446.)

MARCH 10

Examining Your Own Devotion to the Lord

Commit thy way unto the Lord; trust also in him; and he shall bring it to pass.

Ps. 37:5

See also Matt. 4:20; Alma 1:25; D&C 20:37.

As I read and ponder the scriptures and carefully consider the Lord's counsel to His followers in every dispensation of time, it appears to me that the most important thing *every* one of us can do is to examine our own commitment and devotion to the Lord Jesus Christ. We must carefully guard against spiritual apathy and work to maintain the full measure of our loving loyalty to the Lord.

(M. Russell Ballard, "How Is It with Us?" *Ensign*, May 2000, 31.)

MARCH 11

Our Mission in Life

For you shall live by every word that proceedeth forth from the mouth of God.

D&C 84:44

See also Matt. 16:25–26; Rom. 6:12; Alma 12:24.

Life is a mission, not just the sputtering of a candle between a chance lighting and a gust of wind that blows it out forever. . . . While here, we have learning to gain, work to do, service to give. We are here with a marvelous inheritance, a divine endowment. How different this world would be if every person realized that all of his actions have eternal consequences.

(Gordon B. Hinckley, "Pillars of Truth," *Ensign*, January 1994, 2, 4.)

MARCH 12
Finding the Joy of Salvation

And if it so be that you should labor all your days in crying repentance unto this people, and bring, save it be one soul unto me, how great shall be your joy with him in the kingdom of my Father!

And now, if your joy will be great with one soul that you have brought unto me into the kingdom of my Father, how great will be your joy if you should bring many souls unto me!

D&C 18:15–16

See also John 12:47; Mosiah 4:8; Alma 5:21; Hel. 13:6; D&C 53:7.

We find recorded in the Doctrine and Covenants that if we labor all the days of our life and save but one person, great shall be our joy with that person in the life to come. And if that one person is only our dear self, that is the thing that counts.

(Heber J. Grant, *Gospel Standards: Selections from the Sermons and Writings of Heber J. Grant*, comp. G. Homer Durham [Salt Lake City: *Improvement Era*, 1981], 41.)

MARCH 13
Pray for Missionary Experiences

Nevertheless the children of God were commanded that they should gather themselves together oft, and join in fasting and mighty prayer in behalf of the welfare of the souls of those who knew not God.

ALMA 6:6

See also Alma 29:9–10; D&C 31:5; 33:8–11.

We can also pray daily for our own personal missionary experiences. Pray that under the divine management of such things, the missionary opportunity you want is already being prepared in the heart of someone who longs for and looks for what you have.

(Jeffrey R. Holland, "Witnesses unto Me," *Ensign*, May 2001, 14.)

MARCH 14
Honoring the Priesthood

The rights of the priesthood are inseparably connected with the powers of heaven, and . . . the powers of heaven cannot be controlled nor handled only upon the principles of righteousness.

D&C 121:36

See also D&C 13:1; 84:19–21, 33–41.

The Priesthood of the Son of God, which we have in our midst, is a perfect order and system of government, and this alone can deliver the human family from all the evils which now afflict its members, and insure them happiness and felicity hereafter.

(Brigham Young, *Discourses of Brigham Young*, comp. John A. Widtsoe [Salt Lake City: Deseret Book, 1954], 130.)

MARCH 15
Avoiding Apathy

So then because thou art lukewarm, and neither cold nor hot, I will spue thee out of my mouth.

REV. 3:16

See also Ps. 142:4; D&C 58:26.

[There] are Church members who are steeped in lethargy. They neither drink nor commit the sexual sins. They do not gamble nor rob nor kill. They are good citizens and splendid neighbors, but spiritually speaking they seem to be in a long, deep sleep. They are doing nothing seriously wrong except in their failures to do the right things to earn their exaltation.

(Spencer W. Kimball, *The Teachings of Spencer W. Kimball*, ed. Edward L. Kimball [Salt Lake City: Bookcraft, 1982], 149.)

MARCH 16
Reconciling with Others

Go thy way unto thy brother, and first be reconciled to thy brother, and then come unto me with full purpose of heart, and I will receive you.

3 NE. 12:24

See also Matt. 5:23–24; Luke 6:27; Mosiah 26:31.

Harboring an evil thought injures the person who harbors it more than the man against whom he holds ill feeling. Modern psychology emphasizes that truth. If we would have peace, we should banish our enmity for others. Bearing enmity in our hearts injures us and drives peace from our hearts.

(David O. McKay, *The Instructor*, Dec. 1957, 353.)

And now, he imparteth his word by angels unto men, yea, not only men but women also. Now this is not all, little children do have words given unto them many times, which confound the wise and the learned.

ALMA 32:23

See also Ruth 1:16; John 17:19; Rev. 2:19; Mosiah 2:17; D&C 4:2.

I gave much instruction, read in the New Testament, and book of Doctrine and Covenants, concerning the Elect Lady [Emma], and showed that the elect meant to be elected to a certain work, etc., and that the revelation was then fulfilled by Sister Emma's election to the Presidency of the Society, she having previously been ordained to expound the scriptures. Emma was blessed, and her counselors were ordained by Elder John Taylor.

(Joseph Smith, writing in his journal on the founding of the "Female Relief Society of Nauvoo," Thursday, 17 March 1842. *History of the Church of Jesus Christ of Latter-day Saints* 4:552–553.)

MARCH 18

The Key to Strengthening Families

Husbands, love your wives, even as Christ also loved the church, and gave himself for it.

EPH. 5:25

See also 3 Ne. 18:21; D&C 19:34; 20:47.

Strengthening families is our sacred duty as parents, children, extended family members, leaders, teachers, and individual members of the Church. . . . We must understand that each of our children comes with varying gifts and talents. . . . As we teach our children the gospel through word and example, our families are spiritually strengthened and fortified. . . . Whatever the needs of family members may be, we can strengthen our families as we follow the counsel given by prophets. The key to strengthening our families is having the Spirit of the Lord come into our homes. The goal of our families is to be on the strait and narrow path.

(Robert D. Hales, "Strengthening Families: Our Sacred Duty," *Ensign*, May 1999, 32.)

MARCH 19
Understanding the Things of God

By the power of the Spirit our eyes were opened
and our understandings were enlightened, so as to see
and understand the things of God.

D&C 76:12

See also Ps.119:34; Prov. 3:13; Alma 13:28.

To study by faith is to seek understanding and the
Spirit of the Lord through the prayer of faith.

(Ezra Taft Benson, *The Teachings of Ezra Taft Benson* [Salt
Lake City: Bookcraft, 1988], 309.)

MARCH 20

Sacrifice Is an Amazing Principle

And now, my beloved brethren, I would that ye should come unto Christ, who is the Holy One of Israel, and partake of his salvation, and the power of his redemption. Yea, come unto him, and offer your whole souls as an offering unto him, and continue in fasting and praying, and endure to the end; and as the Lord liveth ye will be saved.

OMNI 1:26

See also 1 Pet. 2:5; 3 Ne. 9:20; D&C 132:50.

Sacrifice is an amazing principle. As we willingly give our time and talents and all that we possess, it becomes one of our truest forms of worship. It can develop within us a profound love for each other and our Savior, Jesus Christ. Through sacrifice our hearts can be changed; we live closer to the Spirit and have less of an appetite for things of the world.

(Carol B. Thomas, "Sacrifice: An Eternal Investment," *Ensign*, May 2001, 63.)

MARCH 21
Home Teaching Is a Way to Show Our Faithfulness

But ye will teach them to walk in the ways of truth and soberness; ye will teach them to love one another, and to serve one another.

MOSIAH 4:15

See also 3 Ne. 5:13; D&C 20:7; 38:23; 44:6.

Home teaching is a way to show our faithfulness. What greater opportunity comes to us to show our priesthood faithfulness than to participate in home teaching? In so doing we truly demonstrate our love for our fellowmen by bringing to their homes spiritual and material help.

(Howard W. Hunter, *The Teachings of Howard W. Hunter*, ed. Clyde J. Williams [Salt Lake City: Bookcraft, 1997], 217.)

MARCH 22

Forgiving Others

Wherefore, I say unto you, that ye ought to forgive one another; for he that forgiveth not his brother his trespasses standeth condemned before the Lord; for there remaineth in him the greater sin.

I, the Lord, will forgive whom I will forgive, but of you it is required to forgive all men.

D&C 64:9–10

See also Matt. 6:15; 18:35; Luke 23:34.

It becomes us as a grateful people to reach out with a spirit of forgiveness and an attitude of love and compassion toward those we have felt may have wronged us. We have need of this. The whole world has need of it. It is of the very essence of the gospel of Jesus Christ. He taught it. He exemplified it as none other has exemplified it. . . . None of us is called on to forgive so generously, but each of us is under a divinely spoken obligation to reach out with pardon and mercy.

(Gordon B. Hinckley, *Be Thou an Example* [Salt Lake City: Deseret Book, 1981], 47.)

MARCH 23

Christ-Centered Hope

The hope of the righteous shall be gladness: but the expectation of the wicked shall perish.

PROV. 10:28

See also Jer. 17:9; 1 Cor. 15:19; Alma 32:21.

Real hope, said Paul, is a hope for things that are not seen that are true (see Romans 8:24). Paul accurately linked hopelessness and godlessness as he wrote of those "having no hope, and without God in the world" (Ephesians 2:12). Christ-centered hope, however, is a very specific and particularized hope. It is focused on the great realities of the resurrection, eternal life, a better world, and Christ's triumphant second coming "things as they really will be" (Jacob 4:13).

(Neal A. Maxwell, *Notwithstanding My Weakness* [Salt Lake City: Deseret Book, 1981], 40–41.)

MARCH 24
Dependent upon Heaven

I say unto you that if ye should serve him who has created you from the beginning, and is preserving you from day to day, by lending you breath, that ye may live and move and do according to your own will, and even supporting you from one moment to another—I say, if ye should serve him with all your whole souls yet ye would be unprofitable servants.

MOSIAH 2:21

See also Mosiah 2:19–22; Alma 5:40; D&C 59:21.

Men not unfrequently forget that they are dependent upon heaven for every blessing which they are permitted to enjoy, and that for every opportunity granted them they are to give an account.

(Joseph Smith, *History of The Church of Jesus Christ of Latter-day Saints, 7 vols.*, 2:23–24.)

MARCH 25

But there is a resurrection, therefore the grave hath no victory, and the sting of death is swallowed up in Christ.

MOSIAH 16:8

See also 1 Cor. 6:14; Jacob 4:11; Alma 33:22.

The assurance of resurrection gives us the strength and perspective to endure the mortal challenges faced by each of us and by those we love, such things as the physical, mental, or emotional deficiencies we bring with us at birth or acquire during mortal life. Because of the resurrection, we know that these mortal deficiencies are only temporary!

(Dallin H. Oaks, "Resurrection," *Ensign*, May 2000, 14.)

MARCH 26

Humility Is Essential for Spiritual Knowledge

Let him that is ignorant learn wisdom by humbling himself and calling upon the Lord his God, that his eyes may be opened that he may see, and his ears opened that he may hear.

D&C 136:32

See also Mosiah 3:19; Hel. 3:35; Ether 12:27.

Humility is essential to the acquiring of spiritual knowledge. To be humble is to be teachable. Humility permits you to be tutored by the Spirit and to be taught from sources inspired by the Lord, such as the scriptures. The seeds of personal growth and understanding germinate and flourish in the fertile soil of humility. Their fruit is spiritual knowledge to guide you here and hereafter.

(Richard G. Scott, "Acquiring Spiritual Knowledge," *Ensign*, Nov. 1993, 87.)

MARCH 27
The Redeeming Power of Temple Work

Help thy servants to say, with thy grace assisting them: Thy will be done, O Lord, and not ours.

D&C 109:44

See also D&C 88:119; 109:8; 110.

Oh, I wish many times that the veil were lifted off the face of the Latter-day Saints. I wish we could see and know the things of God as they do who are laboring for the salvation of the human family who are in the spirit world; for if this were so, this whole people, with very few, if any, exceptions, would lose all interest in the riches of the world, and instead thereof their whole desires and labors would be directed to redeem their dead, to perform faithfully the work and mission given us on earth; so that when we ourselves should pass behind the veil and meet with Joseph and the ancient apostles, and others who are watching over us and who are deeply interested in our labors, we might feel satisfied in having done our duty.

(Wilford Woodruff, *The Discourses of Wilford Woodruff*, ed. G. Homer Durham [Salt Lake City: Bookcraft, 1969], 152.)

Create Regimens that Foster Spirituality

And see that all these things are done in wisdom and order; for it is not requisite that a man should run faster than he has strength. And again, it is expedient that he should be diligent, that thereby he might win the prize; therefore, all things must be done in order.

MOSIAH 4:27

See also D&C 88:119; 15-16; 107:84.

My general counsel to you is that we must create regimens that foster spiritual housecleaning—ongoing and continual processes that draw us closer to the Lord our Savior so that we can be numbered among His disciples.

(L. Tom Perry, "Discipleship," *Ensign,* Nov. 2000, 60.)

If so, wo shall come upon you; but if not so, then cast about your eyes and begin to believe in the Son of God, that he will come to redeem his people, and that he shall suffer and die to atone for their sins; and that he shall rise again from the dead, which shall bring to pass the resurrection, that all men shall stand before him, to be judged at the last and judgment day, according to their works.

ALMA 33:22

See also 1 Cor. 6:14; 2 Ne. 2:8–10; D&C 43:18.

The empty tomb that first Easter morning brought the most comforting assurance that can come into man's heart. This was the affirmative answer to the ageless question raised by Job, "If a man die, shall he live again?" (Job 14:14).

(David O. McKay, *Gospel Ideals: Selections from the Discourses of David O. McKay* [Salt Lake City: Improvement Era, 1953], 48.)

MARCH 30

Outward Circumstances Do Not Trouble Me

And whoso receiveth you, there I will be also, for I will go before your face. I will be on your right hand and on your left, and my Spirit shall be in your hearts, and mine angels round about you, to bear you up.

D&C 84:88

See also 1 Ne. 3:7; 17:3; Alma 26:11–12.

Good men have had to endure affliction, privations, trials, and sorrow, it is true. . . . If I am doing right, I am preparing for thrones, principalities, and dominions, resolved by the help of God that no man shall rob me of my crown. With this view of the subject, all the outward circumstances of this life do not trouble me.

(John Taylor, *Journal of Discourses* 8:97, 100.)

MARCH 31
Praying in Faith

If any of you lack wisdom, let him ask of God, that giveth to all men liberally, and upbraideth not; and it shall be given him.

But let him ask in faith, nothing wavering. For he that wavereth is like a wave of the sea driven with the wind and tossed.

JAMES 1:5–6

See also Alma 13:28; Alma 17:3; Hel. 3:35.

Prayer will bring solace and comfort. It has healed sickness, comforted those distressed, and has continued the faithful in paths of righteousness. . . . Our great example in prayer is our Lord and Master Jesus Christ who knew that only through constant supplication and obedience would God the Father manifest His will and release the power for its attainment through man. Truly there is power in prayer.

(Ezra Taft Benson, *The Teachings of Ezra Taft Benson* [Salt Lake City: Bookcraft, 1988], 422.)

APRIL

*The multitude did feel the prints of
the nails in his hands and feet.*

—3 Nephi 11:15

APRIL 1
Following Prophetic Counsel

Believe in the Lord your God, so shall ye be established; believe his prophets, so shall ye prosper.

2 CHR. 20:20

See also Matt. 10:41; Heb. 17:13; D&C 1:38.

As I have pondered the messages of the conference, I have asked myself this question: How can I help others partake of the goodness and blessings of our Heavenly Father? The answer lies in following the direction received from those we sustain as prophets, seers, and revelators, and others of the General Authorities. Let us study their words, spoken under the Spirit of inspiration, and refer to them often.

(Howard W. Hunter, "Follow the Son of God," *Ensign*, Nov. 1994, 87.)

APRIL 2
Work Diligently

Verily I say, men should be anxiously engaged in a good cause, and do many things of their own free will, and bring to pass much righteousness.

D&C 58:27

See also 2 Ne. 5:17; D&C 75:29.

The foundation of self-reliance is hard work. Parents should teach their children that work is the prerequisite to achievement and success in every worthwhile endeavor. Children of legal age should secure productive employment and begin to move away from dependence on parents. None of us should expect others to provide for us anything that we can provide for ourselves.

(Joseph B. Wirthlin, *Finding Peace in Our Lives* [Salt Lake City: Deseret Book, 1995], 44.)

APRIL 3

To Become Pure in Heart

And blessed are all the pure in heart, for they shall see God.

3 NE. 12:8

See also Hel. 3:35; 3 Ne. 19:28; D&C 88:74.

To become pure in heart—to achieve exaltation—we must alter our attitudes and priorities to a condition of spirituality, we must control our thoughts, we must reform our motives, and we must perfect our desires. How can this be done?

(Dallin H. Oaks, *Pure in Heart* [Salt Lake City: Bookcraft, 1988], 140.)

APRIL 4
Achieving Your Full Potential

For if you keep my commandments you shall receive of his fulness, and be glorified in me as I am in the Father; therefore, I say unto you, you shall receive grace for grace.

D&C 93:20

See also Eph. 4:13; 2 Ne. 2:25; D&C 50:24.

For you to achieve your potential, you will need to honor four sacred principles in your lives. These four are:

1. Reverence for Deity.
2. Respecting and honoring family relationships.
3. Reverence for and obedience to the ordinances and covenants of the holy priesthood.
4. Respect for yourself as a son of God.

(James E. Faust, "Them That Honour Me I Will Honour," *Ensign*, May 2001, 45.)

APRIL 5
Embrace the Gospel with Enthusiasm

And they were among the people of Nephi, and also numbered among the people who were of the church of God. And they were also distinguished for their zeal towards God, and also towards men; for they were perfectly honest and upright in all things; and they were firm in the faith of Christ, even unto the end.

Alma 27:27

See also Alma 21:23; D&C 58:27; 75:29.

Well was it said of old, "Where there is no vision, the people perish" (Prov. 29:18). There is no place in this work for those who believe only in the gospel of doom and gloom. The gospel is good news. It is a message of triumph. It is a cause to be embraced with enthusiasm.

(Gordon B. Hinckley, "Stay the Course—Keep the Faith," *Ensign*, Nov. 1995, 70.)

APRIL 6

The Divine Church

Verily I say unto you, that ye are built upon my gospel; therefore ye shall call whatsoever things ye do call, in my name; therefore if ye call upon the Father, for the church, if it be in my name the Father will hear you.

And if it so be that the church is built upon my gospel then will the Father show forth his own works in it.

3 NE. 27:9–10

See also Eph. 4:11–14; D&C 1:30; 20:1; A of F 6.

The Church is divinely organized, and in that organization there is provision for the development and practice of every virtue known, every charity revealed. For this reason and for its promise of eternal life and glory, the gospel, and the Church divinely established for its promulgation, should be nearer and dearer to a follower of Christ than all other things.

(Joseph F. Smith, *Gospel Doctrine: Selections from the Sermons and Writings of Joseph F. Smith*, comp. John A. Widtsoe [Salt Lake City: Deseret Book, 1939], 110.)

APRIL 7

Chastened by the Hand of God

For whom the Lord loveth he chasteneth, and scourgeth every son whom he receiveth.

HEB. 12:6

See also Mosiah 23:21; Hel. 12:3; D&C 95:1–2.

We have been chastened by the hand of God heretofore for not obeying His commands, although we never violated any human law, or transgressed any human precept; yet we have treated lightly His commands, and departed from His ordinances, and the Lord has chastened us sore, and we have felt His arm and kissed the rod; let us be wise in time to come and ever remember that "to obey is better than sacrifice, and to hearken than the fat of rams."

(Joseph Smith, *Teachings of the Prophet Joseph Smith*, sel. Joseph Fielding Smith [Salt Lake City: Deseret Book, 1976], 253.)

APRIL 8
Avoiding Debt

The rich ruleth over the poor, and the borrower is servant to the lender.

PROV. 22:7

See also Luke 14:28; D&C 136:25.

We encourage all to avoid going into debt for speculation purposes. "The love of money is the root of all evil" (1 Tim. 6:10). A proper balance in our money management skills should be the continuing goal of all who would be free of financial bondage.

(Marvin J. Ashton, *Ye Are My Friends* [Salt Lake City: Deseret Book, 1972], 59.)

APRIL 9

Change Lives by Serving

I called you servants for the world's sake, and ye are their servants for my sake.

D&C 93:46

See also Matt. 25:40; Mosiah 4:16; D&C 50:26.

We will discover that those whom we serve, who have felt through our labors the touch of the Master's hand, somehow cannot explain the change which comes into their lives. There is a desire to serve faithfully, to walk humbly, and to live more like the Savior.

(Thomas S. Monson, "To the Rescue," *Ensign*, May 2001, 48.)

APRIL 10
Family History Builds Bridges

For we labor diligently to write, to persuade our children, and also our brethren, to believe in Christ, and to be reconciled to God; for we know that it is by grace that we are saved, after all we can do.

2 NE. 25:23

See also Mal. 4:5–6; D&C 110:7–12; 128:15.

Family history builds bridges between the generations of our families, builds bridges to activity in the Church, and builds bridges to the temple. . . . Family history and temple work have a great power, which lies in their scriptural and divine promise that the hearts of the fathers will turn to the children and those of the children will turn to their fathers.

(Dennis B. Neuenschwander, "Bridges and Eternal Keepsakes," *Ensign*, May 1999, 83.)

APRIL 11

Reverence Invites Revelation

Behold, I say unto you they are made known unto me by the Holy Spirit of God. Behold, I have fasted and prayed many days that I might know these things of myself. And now I do know of myself that they are true; for the Lord God hath made them manifest unto me by his Holy Spirit; and this is the spirit of revelation which is in me.

ALMA 5:46

See also 1 Cor. 12:3; D&C 11:25; 18:34–36.

No one of us can survive in the world of today, much less in what it soon will become, without personal inspiration. The spirit of reverence can and should be evident in every organization in the Church and in the lives of every member.

(Boyd K. Packer, "Reverence Invites Revelation," *Ensign*, Nov. 1991, 23.)

APRIL 12
Obtain Eternal Life through Christ

This is eternal lives—to know the only wise and true God, and Jesus Christ, whom he hath sent. I am he. Receive ye, therefore, my law.

D&C 132:24

See also 2 Ne. 9:39; 33:4; Moro. 7:41.

The great sun is a mighty force in the universe, but we receive the blessings of his rays because they come to us as little beams, which, taken in the aggregate, fill the whole world with sunlight. . . . and so the true Christian life is made up of little Christ–like acts performed this hour, this minute, in the home, in the quorum, in the organization, in the town, wherever our life and acts may be cast.

(David O. McKay, in CR, Oct. 1914, 87–88.)

APRIL 13
Overcoming Temptation

Blessed is the man that endureth temptation: for when he is tried, he shall receive the crown of life, which the Lord hath promised to them that love him.

JAMES 1:12

See also JST Matt. 6:14; 2 Pet. 2:9; 1 Ne. 15:24.

To have strength to overcome temptation is God-like. The strong, the virtuous and the true of every generation have lived pure, clean lives, not because their emotions were less impelling nor because their temptations were fewer but because their will to do was greater and their faith in divine guidance won them strength through prayer that proved their kinship with the great Exemplar who gave us the pattern for the perfect life.

(Harold B. Lee, *Decisions for Successful Living* [Salt Lake City: Deseret Book, 1973], 43.)

APRIL 14

Read the Work of the Lord

And when ye shall receive these things, I would exhort you that ye would ask God, the Eternal Father, in the name of Christ, if these things are not true; and if ye shall ask with a sincere heart, with real intent, having faith in Christ, he will manifest the truth of it unto you, by the power of the Holy Ghost.

And by the power of the Holy Ghost ye may know the truth of all things.

MORO. 10:4–5

See also D&C 33:16; 42:12; A of F 1:18.

There is an inspiration and feeling of peaceful joy and satisfaction which accompany the sincere and prayerful reading of this book [the Book of Mormon]. Its doctrines and literary merit are in keeping with the writings of the Jewish prophets. The sincere student who is willing to put Moroni's promise to the test is forced to say, "Surely this is the work of the Lord and not the work of man, for no man could have written it."

(Joseph Fielding Smith, *Doctrines of Salvation*, 3 vols., ed. Bruce R. McConkie [Salt Lake City: Bookcraft, 1954–56], 3: 209.)

APRIL 15
Actively Participate in Each Day

And we will prove them herewith, to see if they will do all things whatsoever the Lord their God shall command them.

ABR. 3:25

See also 2 Ne. 2:11–30; Alma 12:23–37.

We were sent into this world to learn the meaning and purpose of life by active participation in the exciting drama of human existence. In life, unlike baseball, everyone must participate. There are no benches on which to vegetate and no dugout in which to hibernate.

(Hugh B. Brown, "Be Aware—Beware," [Baccalaureate Address, Brigham Young University, May 24, 1962.])

Gather my saints together unto me; those that have made a covenant with me by sacrifice.

Ps. 50:5

See also Alma 37:27; 3 Ne. 21:22; D&C 136:4.

Sometimes we are tempted to let our lives be governed more by convenience than by covenant. It is not always convenient to live gospel standards and stand up for truth and testify of the Restoration. It usually is not convenient to share the gospel with others. It isn't always convenient to respond to a calling in the Church, especially one that stretches our abilities. Opportunities to serve others in meaningful ways, as we have covenanted to do, rarely come at convenient times. But there is no spiritual power in living by convenience. The power comes as we keep our covenants.

(M. Russell Ballard, "Like a Flame Unquenchable," *Ensign,* May 1999, 86.)

APRIL 17

Put Our Trust in the Lord

O Lord, I have trusted in thee, and I will trust in thee forever. I will not put my trust in the arm of flesh; for I know that cursed is he that putteth his trust in the arm of flesh. Yea, cursed is he that putteth his trust in man or maketh flesh his arm.

2 NE. 4:34

See also Prov. 3:5–7; Alma 36:3.

We must be a tried people. We must walk by faith, putting our trust in the Lord and not, at present, by sight. In this way the leaders of the people of God, as well as the people themselves, have their faith tested.

(George Q. Cannon, *Gospel Truth: Discourses and Writings of President George Q. Cannon*, ed. Jerreld L. Newquist [Salt Lake City: Deseret Book, 1987], 300.)

APRIL 18

Fundamental Belief of Children of God

But we are bound to give thanks alway to God for you, brethren beloved of the Lord, because God hath from the beginning chosen you to salvation through sanctification of the Spirit and belief of the truth.

2 THES. 2:13

See also Alma 46:15; 3 Ne 19:20.

Our belief in God is fundamental. We believe in God the Eternal Father and we believe that Jesus Christ was the manifestation of God in the flesh, his Only Begotten Son; and we believe in the Holy Ghost and the power that it manifests unto those who seek to do the will of our Father in Heaven. This belief is fundamental with us, and it leaves us in the position of children of God. We are the children of our Heavenly Father. He is the Father of our spirits.

(George Albert Smith, *The Teachings of George Albert Smith*, ed. Robert McIntosh and Susan McIntosh [Salt Lake City: Bookcraft, 1996], 2.)

APRIL 19

Righteousness Now and Forever

Lift up your eyes to the heavens, and look upon the earth beneath; for the heavens shall vanish away like smoke, and the earth shall wax old like a garment; and they that dwell therein shall die in like manner. But my salvation shall be forever, and my righteousness shall not be abolished.

2 Ne. 8:6

See also Mosiah 27:24; Alma 7:19; D&C 27:16.

What kind of men and women should we be, as Latter-day Saints, in view of this wonderful knowledge that we possess, that God lives, that Jesus is the Christ, that Joseph Smith is a prophet of God? We should be the most honest, the most virtuous, the most charitable-minded, the best people upon the face of the earth.

(Heber J. *Grant, Gospel Standards: Selections from the Sermons and Writings of Heber J. Grant*, comp. G. Homer Durham [Salt Lake City: Improvement Era, 1981], 4.)

APRIL 20

Love Needs Constant Feeding
with Portions of Love

Owe no man any thing, but to love one another:
for he that loveth another hath fulfilled the law.

ROM. 13:8

See also Matt. 5:44; John 13:34–35; James 2:8.

Love is like a flower, and, like the body, it needs
constant feeding. The mortal body would soon be
emaciated and die if there were not frequent feedings.
The tender flower would wither and die without food
and water. And so love, also, cannot be expected to
last forever unless it is continually fed with portions
of love, the manifestation of esteem and admiration,
the expressions of gratitude, and the consideration of
unselfishness.

(Spencer W. Kimball, "Oneness in Marriage," *Ensign*, Mar.
1977, 5.)

APRIL 21
The Heart and a Willing Mind

Behold, the Lord requireth the heart and a willing mind; and the willing and obedient shall eat the good of the land of Zion in these last days.

D&C 64:34

See also Ex. 35:5; 1 Chr. 28:9; Mosiah 3:19; D&C 97:8.

Welcome the task that takes you beyond yourself.

(Louise Yates Robison, seventh president of the Relief Society; her motto as quoted in Janet Peterson and LaRene Gaunt, *Elect Ladies* [Salt Lake City: Deseret Book, 1990], 124–125.)

APRIL 22
Elevated by the Everlasting Gospel

And I know that he will raise me up at the last day, to dwell with him in glory; yea, and I will praise him forever.

ALMA 36:28

See also John 17:3; D&C 59:2; 76:58; 109:76.

The Lord wishes to establish a closer and more intimate relationship between Himself and us; He wishes to elevate us in the scale of being and intelligence, and this can only be done through the medium of the everlasting gospel which is specially prepared for this purpose.

(Lorenzo Snow, *The Teachings of Lorenzo Snow*, ed. Clyde J. Williams [Salt Lake City: Bookcraft, 1984], 18.)

APRIL 23
Avoiding Envy and Jealousy

A sound heart is the life of the flesh: but envy the rottenness of the bones.

PROV. 14:30

See also Rom. 13:13; 4 Ne. 1:15–16.

There cannot be jealousy. There cannot be meanness. There cannot be any of those things. We must stand a little taller, a little higher, and walk in the direction that He has pointed. "Be ye therefore perfect," said He, "even as your Father which is in heaven is perfect" (Matt. 5:48).

(Gordon B. Hinckley, *Teachings of Gordon B. Hinckley* [Salt Lake City: Deseret Book, 1997], 243.)

APRIL 24

Being Kind, Courteous, and Thoughtful

Finally, be ye all of one mind, having compassion one of another, love as brethren, be pitiful, be courteous.

1 PET. 3:8

See also 3 Ne. 14:12; Moro. 7:45.

If each day we could be kind and courteous and thoughtful, our circle of friends would increase. If we could forget the grumbling and all the other things that are negative, how bright our lives would become. We can do it if we will merely follow the counsel of the Savior, think of him and his life, and lift ourselves by living close to the Spirit and that inspiration.

(Howard W. Hunter, *The Teachings of Howard W. Hunter*, ed. Clyde J. Williams [Salt Lake City: Bookcraft, 1997], 69.)

APRIL 25

Having Charity

For none is acceptable before God, save the meek and lowly in heart; and if a man be meek and lowly in heart, and confesses by the power of the Holy Ghost that Jesus is the Christ, he must needs have charity; for if he have not charity he is nothing; wherefore he must needs have charity.

MORO. 7:44

See also Moro. 7:45–48; 1 Cor. 13; 16:4.

Without faith, hope, and charity the Lord has pointedly said that we "can do nothing" (D&C 18:19), nothing that really matters everlastingly. Furthermore, just as faith precedes the kind of hope being spoken of, we can have neither of these, the prophets tell us, if we are not (even before then) "meek, and lowly of heart" (Moroni 7:43).

(Neal A. Maxwell, *Notwithstanding My Weakness* [Salt Lake City: Deseret Book, 1981], 48.)

APRIL 26
Be the Very Best You Can

And if your eye be single to my glory, your whole bodies shall be filled with light, and there shall be no darkness in you; and that body which is filled with light comprehendeth all things.

D&C 88:67

See also 2 Ne. 31:20; Hel. 10:4–5; Moro. 9:6.

The only thing you need to worry about is striving to be the best you can be. And how do you do that? You keep your eye on the goals that matter most in life, and you move towards them step by step. . . . We don't have to be perfect today. We don't have to be better than someone else. All we have to do is to be the very best we can. . . . He will be at your side, yes, guiding you every step of the way.

(Joseph B. Wirthlin, "One Step after Another," *Ensign*, Nov. 2001, 26–27.)

APRIL 27
Generating Daily Spiritual Light

For they were set to be a light unto the world, and to be the saviors of men.

D&C 103:9

See also D&C 50:23–25; 88:67; 93:36–44.

I became very aware that we cannot store oxygen. We cannot save the air we need to breathe, no matter how hard we try. Moment by moment, breath by breath, our lives are granted to us and are renewed. So it is with spiritual light. It must be renewed in us on a regular basis. We must generate it day by day, thought by thought, and with daily righteous action if we are to keep the darkness of the adversary away.

(Robert D. Hales, "Out of the Darkness into His Marvelous Light," *Ensign*, May 2002, 70–71.)

APRIL 28
Time to Prepare

For behold, this life is the time for men to prepare to meet God; yea, behold the day of this life is the day for men to perform their labors.

ALMA 34:32

See also Alma 42:4.

Time and the ability to labor are the capital stock of the whole world of mankind, and we are all indebted to God for the ability to use time to advantage, and he will require of us a strict account of the disposition we make of this ability; and he will not only require an account of our acts, but our words and thoughts will also be brought into judgment.

(Brigham Young, *Discourses of Brigham Young*, sel. John A. Widtsoe [Salt Lake City: Deseret Book, 1954], 301.)

APRIL 29

Enduring to the End in All Diligence

But he that shall endure unto the end, the same shall be saved.

MATT. 24:13

See also 2 Ne. 31:20; Alma 1:25; Hel. 15:6.

Often one hears trite, sometimes consciously apologetic references to "enduring to the end" as an addition to the first principles and ordinances of the gospel. Nevertheless, the doctrine of faithful endurance is infinitely serious, and it is here declared to be a basic principle of the gospel by the God and Father of us all. "Enduring to the end" is an integral element in the doctrine of Christ, and without it, it would have been better not to have known him.

(Jeffrey R. Holland, *Christ and the New Covenant: The Messianic Message of the Book of Mormon* [Salt Lake City: Deseret Book, 1997], 54.)

APRIL 30
Trust in the Lord

Trust in the Lord with all thine heart; and lean not unto thine own understanding.

In all thy ways acknowledge him, and he shall direct thy paths.

PROV. 3:5–6

See also 2 Ne. 4:34; Alma 36:3.

Absolute trust in the Lord will awaken a desire, at least, to try to live in accordance with Christ's teachings, chief of which is to love, not hate one another.

(David O. McKay, *Gospel Ideals: Selections from the Discourses of David O. McKay* [Salt Lake City: Improvement Era, 1953], 35–36.)

MAY

*Repent ye, for the kingdom of heaven
is at hand.*

—HELAMAN 5:32

MAY 1
The Redeeming Power of Repentance

And there came a voice unto me, saying: Enos, thy sins are forgiven thee, and thou shalt be blessed.

And I, Enos, knew that God could not lie; wherefore, my guilt was swept away.

ENOS 1:5–6

See also Alma 29:9–10; 36:24; D&C 58:42–43.

Are you taking full advantage of the redeeming power of repentance in your life so that you can have greater peace and joy? Feelings of turmoil and despondency often signal a need for repentance. Also the lack of the spiritual direction you seek in your life could result from broken laws. If needed, full repentance will put your life together. It will solve all of the complex spiritual pains that come from transgression.

(Richard G. Scott, "The Path to Peace and Joy," *Ensign*, Nov. 2000, 25.)

MAY 2

Finding Inner Peace

And it came to pass that after they had spoken these words the Spirit of the Lord came upon them, and they were filled with joy, having received a remission of their sins, and having peace of conscience, because of the exceeding faith which they had in Jesus Christ who should come, according to the words which king Benjamin had spoken unto them.

MOSIAH 4:3

See also John 14:27; Rom. 8:6; D&C 19:23.

Inner peace comes only as we maintain the integrity of truth in all aspects of our lives. When we covenant to follow the Lord and obey His commandments, we accept His standards in *every* thought, action, and deed.

(Russell M. Nelson, "Living by Scriptural Guidance," *Ensign*, Nov. 2000, 16.)

MAY 3
Do Not Delay

If ye abide in me, and my words abide in you, ye shall ask what ye will, and it shall be done unto you.

JOHN 15:7

See also James 1:5–6; 5:16; 2 Ne. 4:35.

One of the questions we must ask of our Heavenly Father in private prayer is this: "What have I done today, or not done, which displeases Thee? If I can only know, I will repent with all my heart without delay." That humble prayer will be answered. And the answers will surely include the assurance that asking today was better than waiting to ask tomorrow.

(Henry B. Eyring, "Do Not Delay," *Ensign*, Nov. 1999, 33.)

MAY 4

Stewardship with the Spirit of the Lord

I have fought a good fight, I have finished my course, I have kept the faith.

2 TIM. 4:7

See also D&C 72:3; 78:22; 104:11; 136:27.

Now I like to feel that I have no regrets, that I have done my work as well as I could, that I have tried to have the spirit of the Lord with me at all times.

(Clarissa Smith Williams, quoted in Janet Peterson and LaRene Gaunt, *Elect Ladies* [Salt Lake City: Deseret Book, 1990], 109.)

MAY 5
Our Time to Be Happy Is Now

Happy is the man *that* findeth wisdom, and the man *that* getteth understanding.

PROV. 3:13

See also 1 Ne. 8:10–12; 4 Ne. 1:15–18.

Happiness is not only simple, but it is here for us to experience each day. Happiness is all around us. It can be as immediate as now. Some children said, "Happiness is a big word with flowers all around it." Another said it looks like "a rainbow." "It looks like the sun." We need to remember that despite all of life's challenges, our time to be happy is now.

(Coleen K. Menlove, "Living Happily Ever After," *Ensign*, May 2000, 12.)

MAY 6

Overcoming a Casual Attitude

Search these commandments, for they are true and faithful, and the prophecies and promises which are in them shall all be fulfilled.

D&C 1:37

See also Jacob 7:23; Alma 17:2; D&C 11:22.

I find that when I get casual in my relationships with divinity and when it seems that no divine ear is listening and no divine voice is speaking, that I am far, far away. If I immerse myself in the scriptures the distance narrows and the spirituality returns. I find myself loving more intensely those whom I must love with all my heart and mind and strength, and loving them more, I find it easier to abide their counsel.

(Spencer W. Kimball, *The Teachings of Spencer W. Kimball*, 135.)

MAY 7

Perpetuating Freedom

And for this purpose have I established the Constitution of this land, by the hands of wise men whom I raised up unto this very purpose, and redeemed the land by the shedding of blood.

D&C 101:80

See also D&C 101:77; 134:1–2, 5.

Only in this foreordained land, under its God-inspired Constitution and the resulting environment of freedom, was it possible to have established the restored Church. It is our responsibility to see that this freedom is perpetuated so that the Church may more easily flourish in the future.

(Ezra Taft Benson, *The Teachings of Ezra Taft Benson* [Salt Lake City: Bookcraft, 1988], 620.)

MAY 8
Faithfully Do Your Duty

And now my beloved brethren, I have said these things unto you that I might awaken you to a sense of your duty to God, that ye may walk blameless before him, that ye may walk after the holy order of God, after which ye have been received.

ALMA 7:22

See also Alma 43:46; Hel. 15:5.

Avoid contentions and vain disputes with men of corrupt minds, who do not desire to know the truth. Remember that "it is a day of warning, and not a day of many words." If they receive not your testimony in one place, flee to another, remembering to cast no reflections, nor throw out any bitter sayings. If you do your duty, it will be just as well with you, as though all men embraced the Gospel.

(Joseph Smith, *Teachings of the Prophet Joseph Smith*, sel. Joseph Fielding Smith [Salt Lake City: Deseret Book, 1976], 43.)

MAY 9
Remembering Our Mothers

Yea, they had been taught by their mothers, that if they did not doubt, God would deliver them.

And they rehearsed unto me the words of their mothers, saying: We do not doubt our mothers knew it.

ALMA 56:47–48

See also Matt. 12:49; Alma 57:21.

The true strength that is America's, the true strength of any nation, lies in those qualities of character that have been acquired for the most part by children taught in the quiet, simple, everyday manner of mothers. What Jean Paul Richter once declared of fathers is even more true of mothers—and I paraphrase it just a little to make the point—"What a mother says to her children is not heard by the world, but it will be heard by posterity."

(Gordon B. Hinckley, *Teachings of Gordon B. Hinckley* [Salt Lake City: Deseret Book, 1997], 386.)

MAY 10
Blessed Are the Merciful

And blessed are the merciful, for they shall
obtain mercy.

3 NE. 12:7

See also Luke 6:36; Col. 3:12; Alma 12:33.

Our salvation rests upon the mercy we show to
others. Unkind and cruel words, or wanton acts of
cruelty toward man or beast, even though in seeming
retaliation, disqualify the perpetrator in his claims for
mercy when he has need of mercy in the day of judgment before earthly or heavenly tribunals. Is there
one who has never been wounded by the slander of
another whom he thought to be his friend? Do you
remember the struggle you had to refrain from retri-
bution? Blessed are all you who are merciful for you
shall obtain mercy!

(Harold B. Lee, *Decisions for Successful Living* [Salt Lake
City: Deseret Book, 1973], 60.)

MAY 11
Celebrating Motherhood

Yea, and they did obey and observe to perform every word of command with exactness; yea, and even according to their faith it was done unto them; and I did remember the words which they said unto me that their mothers had taught them.

ALMA 57:21

See also Gen. 3:16; Matt. 15:4; Alma 56:47–48.

I affirm my profound belief that God's greatest creation is womanhood. I also believe that there is no greater good in all the world than motherhood. The influence of a mother in the lives of her children is beyond calculation. Single parents, most of whom are mothers, perform an especially heroic service.

(James E. Faust, *Finding Light in a Dark World* [Salt Lake City: Deseret Book, 1995], 131.)

Honoring Women, Especially Mothers

Honour thy father and thy mother: that thy days may be long upon the land which the Lord thy God giveth thee.

Ex. 20:12

See also Eph. 6:1; Alma 56:48; 57:21.

You young men need to know that you can hardly achieve your highest potential without the influence of good women, particularly your mother and, in a few years, a good wife. Learn now to show respect and gratitude. Remember that your mother is your *mother*. She should not need to issue orders. Her wish, her hope, her hint should provide direction that you would honor. Thank her and express your love for her. And if she is struggling to rear you without your father, you have a double duty to honor her.

(Russell M. Nelson, "Our Sacred Duty to Honor Women," *Ensign*, May 1999, 38.)

MAY 13
The Joy of Womanhood

~~~~~~~~

In like manner also, that women adorn themselves in modest apparel, with shamefacedness and sobriety; not with broided hair, or gold, or pearls, or costly array.

1 TIM. 2:9

See also D&C 42:40; 46:33; 121:45.

Grateful daughters of God guard their bodies carefully, for they know they are the wellspring of life and they reverence life. They don't uncover their bodies to find favor with the world. They walk in modesty to be in favor with their Father in Heaven. For they know He loves them dearly.

(Margaret D. Nadauld, "The Joy of Womanhood," *Ensign,* Nov. 2000, 14.)

MAY 14
Standing for the Kingdom of God

Yea, and are willing to mourn with those that mourn; yea, and comfort those that stand in need of comfort, and to stand as witnesses of God at all times and in all things, and in all places that ye may be in, even until death, that ye may be redeemed of God.

MOSIAH 18:9

See also Alma 6:6; Moro. 6:4.

Every time we strengthen our own testimony or help someone else strengthen theirs, we build the kingdom of God. Every time we mentor a newly baptized sister or befriend a wandering soul without judging her or invite a nonmember family to home evening or give a Book of Mormon to a colleague or lead a family to the temple or stand up for modesty and motherhood or invite the missionaries into our homes or help someone discover the power of the word, we build the kingdom of God.

(Sheri L. Dew, "Stand Tall and Stand Together," *Ensign*, Nov. 2000, 94.)

MAY 15

Perfect Order of the Kingdom

Upon you my fellow servants, in the name of Messiah I confer the Priesthood of Aaron, which holds the keys of the ministering of angels, and of the gospel of repentance, and of baptism by immersion for the remission of sins; and this shall never be taken again from the earth, until the sons of Levi do offer again an offering unto the Lord in righteousness.

D&C 13:1

See also Heb. 5:4; D&C 84:26–28; 107:20.

There is perfect order in the kingdom of God, and he recognizes the authority of his servants. It was for this reason John, who acted under the direction of Peter, James, and John, came to Joseph Smith and Oliver Cowdery and restored the Aaronic Priesthood, which John held in the dispensation of the meridian of time, and which became lost in the great apostasy because of the paganizing and corrupting of the Church of Jesus Christ.

(Joseph Fielding Smith, *Doctrines of Salvation*, 3 vols., ed. Bruce R. McConkie [Salt Lake City: Bookcraft, 1954–56], 3:89.)

MAY 16
Focus and Priorities

For of him unto whom much is given much is required; and he who sins against the greater light shall receive the greater condemnation.

D&C 82:3

See also Alma 34:32; 42:4; D&C 26:1.

We are accountable and will be judged for how we use what we have received. This eternal principle applies to all we have been given. . . . with greatly increased free time and vastly more alternatives for its use, it is prudent to review the fundamental principles that should guide us. Temporal circumstances change, but the eternal laws and principles that should guide our choices never change.

(Dallin H. Oaks, "Focus and Priorities," *Ensign*, May 2001, 82.)

MAY 17

A friend loveth at all times, and a brother is born for adversity.

Prov. 17:17

See also Eph. 2:19; D&C 121:9.

Among life's sweetest blessings is fellowship with men and women whose ideals and aspirations are high and noble. Next to a sense of kinship with God come the helpfulness, encouragement, and inspiration of friends. Friendship is a sacred possession. As air, water, and sunshine to flowers, trees, and verdure, so smiles, sympathy, and love of friends to the daily life of man! "To live, laugh, love one's friends, and be loved by them is to bask in the sunshine of life."

(David O. McKay, *Gospel Ideals: Selections from the Discourses of David O. McKay* [Salt Lake City: Improvement Era, 1953], 253.)

MAY 18
Never Offend a Child

But whoso shall offend one of these little ones which believe in me, it were better for him that a millstone were hanged about his neck, and that he were drowned in the depth of the sea.

MATT. 18:6

See also Matt. 19:14; Mark 7:27; 9:37; Eph. 6:4.

The saddest trend of our day is the alarming increase in child abuse. Much of it occurs within families and involves corrupting the divine innocence that children have from birth. The Savior reserved his harshest condemnation for those who offend little children. He said: "Take heed that ye despise not one of these little ones; for . . . it is not the will of your Father which is in heaven, that one of these little ones should perish" (Matthew 18:10, 14).

(David B. Haight, *A Light unto the World* [Salt Lake City: Deseret Book, 1997], 166–167.)

MAY 19

The Blessings of the Holy Ghost

But the Comforter, which is the Holy Ghost, whom the Father will send in my name, he shall teach you all things, and bring all things to your remembrance, whatsoever I have said unto you.

JOHN 14:26

See also 2 Ne. 32:5; Moro. 10:5; D&C 46:10–33.

Only those who conform to the first ordinances of the Gospel are connected officially with the powers of the Holy Ghost in such a way as to secure added help. A distinct and real power comes to the individual who receives the Holy Ghost. It is as if he had been given a key to a vast and wonderful building which he may enter at his pleasure. However, if the key be unused, the gift is of no value. Man must seek help from the Holy Ghost, if the gift shall be real.

(John A. Widtsoe, *A Rational Theology* [Salt Lake City: Deseret Book, 1937], 96–97.)

MAY 20
Do Good to Others

Fear not to do good, my sons, for whatsoever ye sow, that shall ye also reap; therefore, if ye sow good ye shall also reap good for your reward.

D&C 6:33

See also James 1:22; Mosiah 3:24; 5:15.

We have been sent into the world to do good to others; and in doing good to others we do good to ourselves. . . . There is always opportunity to do good to one another. When you find yourselves a little gloomy, look around you and find somebody that is in a worse plight than yourself; go to him and find out what the trouble is, then try to remove it with the wisdom which the Lord bestows upon you; and the first thing you know, your gloom is gone, you feel light, the Spirit of the Lord is upon you, and everything seems illuminated.

(Lorenzo Snow, in Conference Report, 6 April 1899, 2–3.)

MAY 21

Your Treasures: Wealth and Its Use

Think of your brethren like unto yourselves, and be familiar with all and free with your substance, that they may be rich like unto you.

But before ye seek for riches, seek ye for the kingdom of God.

JACOB 2:17–18

See also 1 Tim. 6:9; 2 Ne. 9:30; Alma 4:6.

I have sought to teach you how to get rich, but I never taught you to neglect your duty; I never instructed you nor taught you to forsake the Lord; and today I would rather not own one farthing, and take my valise in my hand, as I did at the rise of the Church, and travel among the nations of the earth, and beg my bread from door to door, than to neglect my duty and lose the Spirit of Almighty God. If I have wealth and cannot use it to the glory of God and the building up of his Kingdom, I ask the Lord to take it from me.

(Brigham Young, *Discourses of Brigham Young*, sel. John A. Widtsoe [Salt Lake City: Deseret Book, 1954], 229.)

MAY 22

Take Our Modern Prophets Seriously

And he gave some, apostles; and some, prophets;
and some, evangelists; and some, pastors and teachers;

For the perfecting of the saints, for the work of
the ministry, for the edifying of the body of Christ

EPH. 4:11–12

See also 3 Ne. 28:34–35; Ether 11:20; D&C 84:36.

When God gives a message to mankind, it is not
something to be lightly cast aside. Whether He speaks
personally or through His prophets, He Himself said,
it is the same. . . . Shall we not take our modern
prophets seriously and accept them as the servants of
God? Will we choose to follow the wisdom of the
world or the wisdom of these inspired men? Will we
consider worldly deductions of greater value than the
advice of our spiritual leaders?

(Mark E. Petersen, *Why the Religious Life*, 203–206.)

Reflecting Kindness

And be ye kind one to another, tenderhearted, forgiving one another, even as God for Christ's sake hath forgiven you.

EPH. 4:32

See also Moro. 7:45; D&C 121:41–42.

The gospel is a gospel of love and kindness. I pray that the love of the gospel of our Lord will burn in our souls and enrich our lives, that it will cause husbands to be kinder to wives, and wives to be kinder to husbands, parents to children, and children to parents because of the gospel of Jesus Christ, which is a gospel of love and kindness.

(George Albert Smith, *The Teachings of George Albert Smith*, ed. Robert McIntosh and Susan McIntosh [Salt Lake City: Bookcraft, 1996], 136.)

Organizing Your Time

Organize yourselves; prepare every needful thing; and establish a house, even a house of prayer, a house of fasting, a house of faith, a house of learning, a house of glory, a house of order, a house of God.

D&C 88:119

See also Matt. 6:33; Mosiah 4:27; D&C 88:124.

Most people manage their lives by crises. They are driven by external events and circumstances. As each problem arises, they focus on the problem. However, effective time managers are not problem-minded. They are opportunity-minded. They think preventably by using long-range planning. They set their priorities, organize themselves to accomplish these priorities, and then execute their tasks.

(Joseph B. Wirthlin, *Finding Peace in Our Lives* [Salt Lake City: Deseret Book, 1995], 224.)

MAY 25

Choosing to Be Steadfast

Wherefore, ye must press forward with a steadfastness in Christ, having a perfect brightness of hope, and a love of God and of all men. Wherefore, if ye shall press forward, feasting upon the word of Christ, and endure to the end, behold, thus saith the Father: Ye shall have eternal life.

2 NE. 31:20

See also Mosiah 4:11; 5:15; D&C 31:9.

We choose to be steadfast and immovable in our faith because of the promises of eternal glory, eternal increase, and continued family relationships in the celestial kingdom. We love our families and know that our greatest joy and peace come to us as we watch each family member face the tests of life and make righteous choices to overcome the world.

(Mary Ellen Smoot, "Steadfast and Immovable," *Ensign*, Nov. 2001, 91.)

MAY 26

A Lovely Daughter of God

Who can find a virtuous woman? for her price is far above rubies.

PROV. 31:10

See also 1 Tim. 4:12; 2 Tim. 2:22; D&C 25:2.

Of all the creations of the Almighty, there is none more beautiful, none more inspiring than a lovely daughter of God who walks in virtue with an understanding of why she should do so, who honors and respects her body as a thing sacred and divine, who cultivates her mind and constantly enlarges the horizon of her understanding, who nurtures her spirit with everlasting truth.

(Gordon B. Hinckley, "Our Responsibility to Our Young Women," *Ensign*, Sept. 1988, 11.)

MAY 27

Everyone Is Important

So God created man in his own image, in the image of God created he him; male and female created he them.

GEN. 1:27

See also John 3:16; 2 Ne. 26:24; Moses 1:39.

God has given each of us one or more special talents. Socrates made the famous statement, 'The unexamined life is not worth living' ("Apology," *The Dialogues of Plato*, trans. Benjamin Jowett, Chicago: *Encyclopaedia Britannica*, 1952, 210). It is up to each of us to search for and build upon the gifts which God has given. We must remember that each of us is made in the image of God, that there are no unimportant persons. Everyone matters to God and to his fellowmen.

(Marvin J. Ashton, "There Are Many Gifts," *Ensign*, Nov. 1987, 20–21.)

MAY 28

Forbear One with Another

But I say unto you, Love your enemies, bless them that curse you, do good to them that hate you, and pray for them which despitefully use you, and persecute you.

MATT. 5:44

See also Matt. 5:7, 9–10.

Brethren, bear and forbear one with another, for so the Lord does with us. Pray for your enemies in the Church and curse not your foes without: for vengeance is mine, saith the Lord, and I will repay. To every ordained member, and to all, we say, be merciful and you shall find mercy.

(Joseph Smith, *Discourses of the Prophet Joseph Smith*, comp. Alma P. Burton [Salt Lake City: Deseret Book, 1977], 213.)

MAY 29

Think to Thank

Giving thanks always for all things unto God
and the Father in the name of our Lord Jesus Christ.

Eph. 5:20

See also Col. 2:7; Mosiah 26:39; D&C 59:7.

Gracias, danke, merci—whatever language is spoken, "thank you" frequently expressed will cheer your
spirit, broaden your friendships, and lift your lives to
a higher pathway as you journey toward perfection.
There is a simplicity—even a sincerity—when "thank
you" is spoken.

(Thomas S. Monson, "Think to Thank," *Ensign*, Nov. 1998,
17.)

MAY 30
Your Good Example Helps Others

And the Lord said unto them also: Go forth among the Lamanites, thy brethren, and establish my word; yet ye shall be patient in long-suffering and afflictions, that ye may show forth good examples unto them in me, and I will make an instrument of thee in my hands unto the salvation of many souls.

ALMA 17:11

See also 2 Ne. 31:9, 16; Alma 39:1.

When you keep the commandments and follow the Savior's example, it's like holding up a light. Your good example helps others to find their way in a darkening world. It takes courage to do what you know to be right even when it is hard, very hard. But you will never lose your courage unless you choose to.

(Ardeth G. Kapp, "Stand for Truth and Righteousnes," *Ensign*, Nov. 1988, 93–95.)

MAY 31
Bearing Testimony

Yea, and are willing to mourn with those that mourn; yea, and comfort those that stand in need of comfort, and to stand as witnesses of God at all times and in all things, and in all places that ye may be in, even until death, that ye may be redeemed of God, and be numbered with those of the first resurrection, that ye may have eternal life.

MOSIAH 18:9

See also Alma 5:45–47; 30:41; Hel. 9:39.

While a witness may come from hearing a testimony borne by another, I am convinced that *the* witness comes when the Spirit of the Lord falls upon a man or woman when he or she is bearing testimony personally. Teach them to bear testimony. If they don't have a testimony it may come when they start bearing it.

(Boyd K. Packer, *Let Not Your Heart Be Troubled* [Salt Lake City: Bookcraft, 1991], 153.)

JUNE

The eye hath never seen, neither hath the ear heard . . . so great and marvelous things as we saw and heard . . .

—3 Nephi 17:16

JUNE 1

The Light of the Priesthood

Therefore, in the ordinances thereof, the power of godliness is manifest.

D&C 84:20

See also Mosiah 13:6; D&C 90:11; 113:8.

A loving Father in Heaven has sent his sons and daughters here to mortality to gain experience and to be tested. He has provided the way back to him and has given us enough spiritual light to see our way. The priesthood of God gives light to his children in this dark and troubled world. Through priesthood power we can receive the gift of the Holy Ghost to lead us to truth, testimony, and revelation. This gift is available on an equal basis to men, women, and children. Through the blessings of the priesthood, we can be equipped with "the whole armour of God, that [we] may be able to stand against the wiles of the devil" (see Eph. 6:11–18). This protection is available to every one of us.

(Robert D. Hales, "Blessings of the Priesthood," *Ensign*, Nov. 1995, 32.)

JUNE 2

The Ideal Family Fulfillment

And Adam and Eve blessed the name of God, and they made all things known unto their sons and their daughters.

MOSES 5:12

See also D&C 58:26–29; 68:25–28; Moses 5:16.

Throughout your life on earth, seek diligently to fulfill the fundamental purposes of this life *through the ideal family.* While you may not have yet reached that ideal, do all you can through obedience and faith in the Lord to consistently draw as close to it as you are able. Let nothing dissuade you from that objective. If it requires fundamental changes in your personal life, make them.

(Richard G. Scott, "First Things First," *Ensign*, May 2001, 6.)

JUNE 3
Justice and Mercy

For behold, justice exerciseth all his demands, and also mercy claimeth all which is her own; and thus, none but the truly penitent are saved.

ALMA 42:24

See also Alma 12:15; 41:3; D&C 46:15.

Part of the basis for demonstrating the perfection of God's justice and mercy will thus be the cumulative record which we ourselves will have made (see Alma 41:7). Out of this we can be justly judged, a judgment that will include our compliance with outward gospel ordinances with all their respective covenants.

(Neal A. Maxwell, *Lord, Increase Our Faith* [Salt Lake City: Bookcraft, 1994], 75.)

JUNE 4
Fathers of Charity

And, ye fathers, provoke not your children to wrath: but bring them up in the nurture and admonition of the Lord.

EPH. 6:4

See also 1 Tim. 3:4; Heb. 12:9; D&C 93:42–4.

As fathers of our homes, we have a serious responsibility to assume leadership in the home. We must create homes where the Spirit of the Lord can abide. . . . We must be more Christlike in our attitude and behavior than what we see in the world. We should be as charitable and considerate with our loved ones as Christ is with us. He is kind, loving, and patient with each of us. Should we not reciprocate the same love to our wives and children?

(Ezra Taft Benson, *Come unto Christ* [Salt Lake City: Deseret Book, 1983], 53.)

JUNE 5

Reacting Responsibly to Circumstances

But behold, because of the exceedingly great length of the war between the Nephites and the Lamanites many had become hardened, because of the exceedingly great length of the war; and many were softened because of their afflictions, insomuch that they did humble themselves before God, even in the depth of humility.

ALMA 62:41

See also 2 Ne. 2:1–4; 4:20–35; Alma 33:11.

Difficult circumstances do not relieve us of responsibility. No one should deny the importance of circumstances, yet in the final analysis the most important thing is how we react to the circumstances. I have seen poverty produce quite different results in people; some it embitters, so that in their self-pity they simply give up and abandon the future; others it challenges, so that in their determination to succeed in spite of obstacles they grow into capable, powerful people. Even if they never escape from economic stress, they develop inner resources that we associate with progress toward a Christlike character.

(Spencer W. Kimball, *The Teachings of Spencer W. Kimball,* ed. Edward L. Kimball [Salt Lake City: Bookcraft, 1982], 161.)

JUNE 6

Love as a Covenant

A new commandment I give unto you, That ye love one another; as I have loved you, that ye also love one another.

By this shall all men know that ye are my disciples, if ye have love one to another.

JOHN 13:34–35

See also John 14:15; Rom. 12:10; 1 Pet. 1:22.

Too many believe that love is a condition, a feeling that involves one hundred percent of the heart, something that happens to you. They disassociate love from the mind and, therefore, from agency. In commanding us to love, the Lord refers to something much deeper than romance—a love that is the most profound form of loyalty. He is teaching us that love is something more than feelings of the heart; it is also a covenant we keep with soul and mind.

(Lynn G. Robbins, "Agency and Love in Marriage," *Ensign,* Oct. 2000, 16.)

JUNE 7
Teach Our Youth

Let the word of Christ dwell in you richly in all wisdom; teaching and admonishing one another in psalms and hymns and spiritual songs, singing with grace in your hearts to the Lord.

COL. 3:16

See also Mosiah 4:15; Alma 39:12; D&C 68:28.

There is a desperate need for parents, leaders, and teachers to help our youth learn to understand, love, value, and live the standards of the gospel. Parents and youth must stand together in defense against a clever and devious adversary. We must be just as dedicated, effective, and determined in our efforts to live the gospel as he is in his efforts to destroy it—and us.

(M. Russell Ballard, "Like a Flame Unquenchable," *Ensign*, May 1999, 85.)

JUNE 8

Joy of Fatherhood

I have no greater joy than to hear that my children walk in truth.

3 JOHN 1:4

See also 1 Tim. 3:4; Heb. 12:9; D&C 93:42–43.

It is a tremendous responsibility to be a father in The Church of Jesus Christ of Latter-day Saints. It is a wonderful responsibility to be a man who stands at the head of his family as one who holds the priesthood of God with authority to speak in the name of God. Fathers, are you the kind of father you ought to be?

(Gordon B. Hinckley, *Teachings of Gordon B. Hinckley* [Salt Lake City: Deseret Book, 1997], 219–220.)

JUNE 9
Serving with Love

But ye will teach them to walk in the ways of truth and soberness; ye will teach them to love one another, and to serve one another.

MOSIAH 4:15

See also Matt. 25:40; D&C 81:5.

Live in all things outside yourself by love. As you serve others, the children around you, your father, your mother, your associates, ever striving to make yourself and the world better, then will your souls grow in wisdom. Therein you will find the guide to the happy life.

(David O. McKay, *Pathways to Happiness* [Salt Lake City: Bookcraft, 1957], 161.)

JUNE 10
Unity of the Saints

So we, being many, are one body in Christ, and every one members one of another.

ROM. 12:5

See also John 13:34–35; 2 Cor. 13:11; 1 Pet. 3:8.

The unity of the Saints is unique and powerful. . . . We enjoy that unity through love. We can neither purchase nor force it. Our method is to "persuade . . . and bless with wisdom, love, and light . . . but never force the human mind." To the extent we operate in other ways, we diminish our right to be recognized as disciples of Christ.

(John K. Carmack, "United in Love and Testimony," *Ensign*, May 2001, 76.)

JUNE 11
Relinquish Materialism

Love not the world, neither the things that are in the world. If any man love the world, the love of the Father is not in him.

1 Jn. 2:15

See also 1 Ne. 22:23; 2 Ne. 9:30; Alma 4:8; 5:37.

It is necessary to say a word about what is "enough income." This is a materialistic world, and Latter-day Saints must be careful not to confuse luxuries with necessities. An adequate income allows us to provide for the basic requirements of life. There are some who unwisely aspire to self-indulgent luxuries that often lead them away from complete commitment to the gospel of our Savior.

(Howard W. Hunter, *The Teachings of Howard W. Hunter*, ed. Clyde J. Williams [Salt Lake City: Bookcraft, 1997], 162.)

JUNE 12

You Are Never Alone

Teaching them to observe all things whatsoever I have commanded you: and, lo, I am with you alway, even unto the end of the world. Amen.

MATT. 28:20

See also D&C 62:9; 75:14; 105:41.

Your responsibility to endure is uniquely yours. But you are never alone. I testify that the lifting power of the Lord can be yours if you will "come unto Christ" and "be perfected in him." You will "deny yourselves of all ungodliness." And you will "love God with all your might, mind and strength" (Moroni 10:32).

(Russell M. Nelson, "Endure and Be Lifted Up," *Ensign*, May 1997, 72.)

JUNE 13

Fathers Arise

Behold, it came to pass that I, Enos, knowing my father that he was a just man—for he taught me in his language, and also in the nurture and admonition of the Lord—and blessed be the name of my God for it.

ENOS 1:1

See also 1 Ne. 1:1; Enos 1:3; Alma 36–42.

As a father, I wonder if I and all other fathers could do more to build a sweeter, stronger relationship with our sons and daughters here on earth. Dads, is it too bold to hope that our children might have some small portion of the feeling for us that the Divine Son felt for His Father? Might we earn more of that love by trying to be more of what God was to His child?

(Jeffrey R. Holland, "The Hands of the Fathers," *Ensign*, May 1999, 14.)

JUNE 14

Do You Want to Know the Truth?

And by the power of the Holy Ghost ye may know the truth of all things.

MORO. 10:5

See also Alma 24:30; Ether 4:11–12; D&C 4:7.

Do you want to know the truth of the holy scriptures? Do you wish to break the barriers that separate mortals from the knowledge of eternal verities? Do you wish to know—really know—the truth? Then follow Moroni's counsel and you will surely find what you seek. Be sincere. Study. Ponder. Pray sincerely, having faith.

(Joseph B. Wirthlin, "Pure Testimony," *Ensign*, Nov. 2000, 22.)

JUNE 15
Blessings of the Priesthood

And without the ordinances thereof, and the authority of the priesthood, the power of godliness is not manifest unto men in the flesh.

D&C 84:21

See also Mark 3:15; 1 Ne. 17:48; D&C 121:36.

I have reached the conclusion in my own mind that no man, however great his intellectual attainments, however vast and far-reaching his service may be, arrives at the full measure of his sonship and the manhood the Lord intended him to have, without the investiture of the Holy Priesthood, and with that appreciation, my brethren, I have given thanks to the Lord all my life for this marvelous blessing which has come to me.

(Stephen L. Richards, in Conference Report, Oct. 1955, 88.)

JUNE 16
Be Cheerful

Therefore, dearly beloved brethren, let us cheerfully do all things that lie in our power; and then may we stand still, with the utmost assurance, to see the salvation of God, and for his arm to be revealed.

D&C 123:17

See also Prov. 15:13; 17:22; 2 Cor. 9:7.

Be cheerful in all that you do. Live joyfully. Live happily. Live enthusiastically, knowing that God does not dwell in gloom and melancholy, but in light and love.

(Ezra Taft Benson, *God, Family, Country: Our Three Great Loyalties* [Salt Lake City: Deseret Book, 1974], 4.)

JUNE 17

Marriage As the First Priority

Husbands, love your wives, even as Christ also loved the church, and gave himself for it;

That he might sanctify and cleanse it with the washing of water by the word,

That he might present it to himself a glorious church, not having spot, or wrinkle, or any such thing; but that it should be holy and without blemish.

So ought men to love their wives as their own bodies. He that loveth his wife loveth himself.

EPH. 5:25–28

See also Prov. 12:4; 1 Cor. 11:11; D&C 42:22.

I urge the husbands and fathers of this Church to be the kind of a man your wife would not want to be without. I urge the sisters of this Church to be patient, loving, and understanding with their husbands. Those who enter into marriage should be fully prepared to establish their marriage as the first priority in their lives.

(James E. Faust, "Father, Come Home," *Ensign*, May 1993, 35.)

JUNE 18
The Power of Teaching Doctrine

But behold, if ye will awake and arouse your faculties, even to an experiment upon my words, and exercise a particle of faith, yea, even if ye can no more than desire to believe, let this desire work in you, even until ye believe in a manner that ye can give place for a portion of my words.

ALMA 32:27

See also Acts 2:42; Alma 31:5; Hel. 3:35.

The word of God is the doctrine taught by Jesus Christ and by His prophets. . . . The need to open eyes and hearts tells us how we must teach doctrine. Doctrine gains its power as the Holy Ghost confirms that it is true. We prepare those we teach, as best we can, to receive the quiet promptings of the still, small voice. . . . Truth can prepare its own way. Simply hearing the words of doctrine can plant the seed of faith in the heart. And even a tiny seed of faith in Jesus Christ invites the Spirit.

(Henry B. Eyring, "The Power of Teaching Doctrine," *Ensign*, May 1999, 73.)

JUNE 19

Making Choices with Trusting Faith

Trust in the Lord with all thine heart; and lean not unto thine own understanding.

In all thy ways acknowledge him, and he shall direct thy paths.

PROV. 3:5–6

See also Ps. 2:12; 56:4; Prov. 16:20.

[A testimony] is the very essence of character woven from threads born of countless correct decisions. These choices are made with trusting faith in things that are believed and, at least initially, are not seen (Ether 12:6). A strong testimony gives peace, comfort, and assurance. It generates the conviction that as the teachings of the Savior are consistently obeyed, life will be beautiful, the future secure, and there will be capacity to overcome the challenges that cross our path.

(Richard G. Scott, "The Power of a Strong Testimony," *Ensign*, Nov. 2001, 87.)

JUNE 20
Desire Righteousness

But behold, if ye will awake and arouse your faculties, even to an experiment upon my words, and exercise a particle of faith, yea, even if ye can no more than desire to believe, let this desire work in you, even until ye believe in a manner that ye can give place for a portion of my words.

ALMA 32:27

See also Rom. 10:1; 3 Ne. 14:7.

The scriptures say that when we desire righteousness our "heart is right" with God. The Psalmist condemned the people of ancient Israel because "their heart was not right with [God]" (Ps. 78:37).

(Dallin H. Oaks, *Pure in Heart* [Salt Lake City: Bookcraft, 1988], 4.)

JUNE 21
Trust in the Lord for Forgiveness

And now behold, I ask of you, my brethren of the church, have ye spiritually been born of God? Have ye received his image in your countenances? Have ye experienced this mighty change in your hearts?

ALMA 5:14

See also 2 Ne. 1:15; 25:23; Alma 32:27; Hel. 15:7.

Spiritual conversion is preceded by an intense desire for change and an admission that we need divine help. Only those who humbly open their hearts have the courage to admit error and place their trust in the Lord for forgiveness and redemption.

(J. Richard Clarke, "The Lord of Life," *Ensign*, May 1993, 9.)

JUNE 22

Dealing with Anger

But I say unto you, that whosoever is angry with his brother shall be in danger of his judgment. And whosoever shall say to his brother, Raca, shall be in danger of the council; and whosoever shall say, Thou fool, shall be in danger of hell fire.

3 NE. 12:22

See also Matt. 5:23–24; 10; 18:6; 2 Ne. 4:29.

Anger is not an expression of strength. It is an indication of one's inability to control his thoughts, words, his emotions. Of course it is easy to get angry. When the weakness of anger takes over, the strength of reason leaves. Cultivate within yourselves the mighty power of self-discipline.

(Gordon B. Hinckley "Our Solemn Responsibilities," *Ensign,* November 1991, 51.)

JUNE 23
Becoming Humble

And no one can assist in this work except he shall be humble and full of love, having faith, hope, and charity, being temperate in all things, whatsoever shall be entrusted to his care.

D&C 12:8

See also D&C 112:10; Alma 32:13–15.

How does one get humble? To me, one must constantly be reminded of his dependence. On whom dependent? On the Lord. How remind one's self? By real, constant, worshipful, grateful prayer. . . . Humility is teachableness—an ability to realize that all virtues and abilities are not concentrated in one's self.

(Spencer W. Kimball, *The Teachings of Spencer W. Kimball*, ed. Edward L. Kimball [Salt Lake City: Bookcraft, 1982], 233.)

JUNE 24

Wherefore, may God raise you from death by the power of the resurrection, and also from everlasting death by the power of the atonement, that ye may be received into the eternal kingdom of God, that ye may praise him through grace divine. Amen.

2 NE. 10:25

See also Alma 34:8; Moro. 7:41; D&C 29:1.

It was difficult for Jesus to accomplish the Atonement. Jesus, the Son of God, was sent into the world to make it possible for you and me to receive these extraordinary blessings. He had to make a great sacrifice. It required all the power that He had and all the faith that He could summon for Him to accomplish that which the Father required of Him.

(Lorenzo Snow, *The Teachings of Lorenzo Snow,* ed. Clyde J. Williams [Salt Lake City: Bookcraft, 1984], 98).

JUNE 25
Three Elements of Integrity

Righteous lips are the delight of kings; and they love him that speaketh right.

PROV. 16:13

See also Rom. 13:13; 2 Cor. 13:7; 2 Ne. 9:34.

Indeed, I am more concerned about the failure of our moral computers of honesty, integrity, decency, civility, and sexual purity. How many people today are truly incorruptible? . . . This breakdown of moral values is happening because we are separating the teachings of God from personal conduct. An honorable man or woman will personally commit to live up to certain self-imposed expectations, with no need of an outside check or control. I would hope that we can load our moral computers with three elements of integrity: dealing justly with oneself, dealing justly with others, and recognizing the law of the harvest.

(James E. Faust, "This Is Our Day," *Ensign*, May 1999, 17.)

JUNE 26
Mastering Self-Control

And when he had called the people unto him with his disciples also, he said unto them, Whosoever will come after me, let him deny himself, and take up his cross, and follow me.

MARK 8:34

See also 1 Cor. 9:25.

Self-control, self-mastery, is one of the fundamental purposes of life. You see it exemplified in the life of the Savior on the Mount of Temptation when he resisted the tempter. There is a lesson of life to us all in the temptation which he withstood. Satan tauntingly tempts us, and unless we resist and have in mind a higher goal than the mere indulgence or gratification of the physical, we are going to weaken, and the tempter will gain in strength.

(David O. McKay, *Man May Know for Himself: Teachings of President David O. McKay*, comp. Clare Middlemiss [Salt Lake City: Deseret Book, 1967], 19.)

JUNE 27
Hope and Knowledge Support the Soul

Now the God of hope fill you with all joy and peace in believing, that ye may abound in hope, through the power of the Holy Ghost.

ROM. 15:13

See also 1 John 3:3; 2 Ne. 31:20; Ether 12:4.

Though the thunders might roll and lightnings flash, and earthquakes bellow, and war gather thick around, yet this hope and knowledge would support the soul in every hour of trial, trouble and tribulation. Then knowledge through our Lord and Savior Jesus Christ is the grand key that unlocks the glories and mysteries of the kingdom of heaven.

(Joseph Smith, *Teachings of the Prophet Joseph Smith*, sel. Joseph Fielding Smith [Salt Lake City: Deseret Book, 1976], 298.)

JUNE 28
Bearing Record of Jesus Christ

I have reason to bless my God and my Savior Jesus Christ, that he brought our fathers out of the land of Jerusalem, (and no one knew it save it were himself and those whom he brought out of that land) and that he hath given me and my people so much knowledge unto the salvation of our souls.

3 Ne. 5:20

See also Moro. 7:2; D&C 135:3.

The Book of Mormon bears record of the personality and reality of Jesus Christ, both by prophecy uttered hundreds of years before he was born and by recording his personal appearance among the ancient people on this American continent. In this sacred volume we have his words recorded and the testimony of witnesses who saw him and unto whom he ministered after his resurrection.

(Joseph Fielding *Smith, Doctrines of Salvation*, 3 vols., ed. Bruce R. McConkie [Salt Lake City: Bookcraft, 1954–56], 1:35.)

JUNE 29
Sacrifice Brings Blessings

And whosoever shall compel thee to go a mile, go with him twain.

3 NE. 12:41

See also 3 Ne. 9:20; D&C 132:9, 50.

The Lord requires sacrifice, meaning something above and beyond the minimum. The Master spoke of the "second mile" and told us to go there (see Matt. 5:41). Why? Because he wants to bless us. So he put all the blessings in the second mile, but we must go where they are before we get them.

(Hartman Rector, Jr., in Conference Report, Mar. 31, 1979, 42.)

JUNE 30
Resolution in Our Hearts

Commit thy way unto the Lord; trust also in him; and he shall bring it to pass.

Ps. 37:5

See also Matt. 5:22–23; 7:12; Moro. 7:45.

Let us return to our homes with resolution in our hearts to do a little better than we have done in the past. We can all be a little kinder, a little more generous, a little more thoughtful of one another. We can be a little more tolerant and friendly to those not of our faith, going out of our way to show our respect for them. We cannot afford to be arrogant or self-righteous. It is our obligation to reach out in helpfulness, not only to our own but to all others as well. Their interest in and respect for this Church will increase as we do so.

(Gordon B. Hinckley, "Thanks to the Lord for His Blessings," *Ensign*, May 1999, 88.)

JULY

*And the Lord said . . .
I give unto you power that ye shall
baptize this people . . .*

—3 Nephi 11:21

JULY 1

Love Our Children

And, ye fathers, provoke not your children to wrath: but bring them up in the nurture and admonition of the Lord.

EPH. 6:4

See also Matt. 18:6, 19:14; Mark 7:27; 9:37.

Children should not be ignored or neglected. They absolutely must not be abused or molested. Children must not be abandoned or estranged by divorce. Parents are responsible to provide for their children.

(Boyd K. Packer, "Children," *Ensign*, May 2002, 8.)

JULY 2

Preserving Our Constitution

We believe that no government can exist in peace, except such laws are framed and held inviolate as will secure to each individual the free exercise of conscience, the right and control of property, and the protection of life.

D&C 134:2

See also Ether 8:22; D&C 98:5; 134:5–6.

You must keep your honor. You cannot yet speak officially for the country, but you can become informed. You can speak your mind. You may think you can do little about the national economy or the actions of our government and the moral weakness all about us, but we must all remember that the Lord has placed great responsibilities upon the elders of Israel in the preservation of our Constitution.

(Ezra Taft Benson, *The Teachings of Ezra Taft Benson* [Salt Lake City: Bookcraft, 1988], 622.)

JULY 3

Keeping a Journal

For we labor diligently to write, to persuade our children, and also our brethren, to believe in Christ, and to be reconciled to God; for we know that it is by grace that we are saved, after all we can do.

2 NE. 25:23

See also 1 Ne. 1:1; Moro. 7:1; 9:1.

The keeping of journals, said President Kimball, is tied to the keeping of the fifth great commandment. Genealogical work is clearly interlaced with temple work, which, in turn, is tied to the vital ordinances necessary to our own basic salvation. The vows we have made are before us as we do work for our kindred dead.

(Neal A. Maxwell, *Notwithstanding My Weakness* [Salt Lake City: Deseret Book, 1981], 19.)

JULY 4

Nurturing Freedom

And it came to pass that he rent his coat; and he took a piece thereof, and wrote upon it—In memory of our God, our religion, and freedom, and our peace, our wives, and our children—and he fastened it upon the end of a pole.

ALMA 46:12

See also Alma 43:48–50; 48:11; 50:39.

Freedom should be our constant goal, not only for ourselves but for all men. What we seek is not a fitful, tenuous freedom based on compromise of principle and expediency, but a real and lasting freedom founded on the recognition of human rights. True freedom springs from within. It is born in the hearts of men and nurtured on more freedom. If we have freedom as our goal, we have a measuring stick against which to gauge our problems, our actions, and the trend of our times.

(Ezra Taft Benson, *The Teachings of Ezra Taft Benson* [Salt Lake City: Bookcraft, 1988], 654–55.)

JULY 5

God Loves Each One of Us

But behold, the Lord hath redeemed my soul from hell; I have beheld his glory, and I am encircled about eternally in the arms of his love.

2 NE. 1:15

See also John 3:16; 1 Jn. 3:1; 4 Ne. 1:15–18.

No one of us is less treasured or cherished of God than another. I testify that He loves each of us—insecurities, anxieties, self-image, and all. He doesn't measure our talents or our looks; He doesn't measure our professions or our possessions. He cheers on *every* runner, calling out that the race is against sin, *not* against each other. I know that if we will be faithful, there is a perfectly tailored robe of righteousness ready and waiting for *everyone,* "robes . . . made . . . white in the blood of the Lamb."

(Jeffrey R. Holland, "The Other Prodigal," *Ensign,* May 2002, 64.)

Know ye not that ye are the temple of God, and that the Spirit of God dwelleth in you?

If any man defile the temple of God, him shall God destroy; for the temple of God is holy, which temple ye are.

1 COR. 3:16–17

See also Isa. 52:11; 1 Ne. 10:21; D&C 97:21.

Pornography, though billed by Satan as entertainment, is a deeply poisonous, deceptive snake that lies coiled up in magazines, the Internet, and the television. Pornography destroys self-esteem and weakens self-discipline.

(David E. Sorensen, "You Can't Pet a Rattlesnake," *Ensign*, May 2001, 41.)

JULY 7

Adversity: An Inevitable Part of Life

For it must needs be, that there is an opposition in all things. If not so, my first-born in the wilderness, righteousness could not be brought to pass, neither wickedness, neither holiness nor misery, neither good nor bad. Wherefore, all things must needs be a compound in one.

2 NE. 2:11

See also Isa. 30:20; Rom. 12:12; D&C 122:7.

The Lord has not promised us freedom from adversity and affliction. Instead, he has given us the avenue of communication known as prayer, whereby we might humble ourselves and seek his help and divine guidance.

(Spencer W. Kimball, *The Teachings of Spencer W. Kimball*, ed. Edward L. Kimball [Salt Lake City: Bookcraft, 1982], 115.)

JULY 8

Paying an Honest Tithe

Will a man rob God? Yet ye have robbed me.
But ye say, Wherein have we robbed thee? In tithes
and offerings.

MAL. 3:8

See also D&C 64:23; 119.

The law of tithing is the law of revenue for The
Church of Jesus Christ of Latter-day Saints. Without
it, it would be impossible to carry on the purposes of
the Lord.

(Joseph F. Smith, *Gospel Doctrine: Selections from the Sermons
and Writings of Joseph F. Smith*, comp. John A. Widtsoe [Salt Lake
City: Deseret Book, 1939], 226.)

JULY 9
Kneeling Together in Prayer

Pray always, and I will pour out my Spirit upon you, and great shall be your blessing—yea, even more than if you should obtain treasures of earth and corruptibleness to the extent thereof.

D&C 19:38

See also Luke 18:1; Mosiah 4:11; Alma 34:19.

I know of no single practice that will have a more salutary effect upon your lives than the practice of kneeling together as you begin and close each day. Somehow the little storms that seem to afflict every marriage are dissipated when, kneeling before the Lord, you thank him for one another, in the presence of one another, and then together invoke his blessings upon your lives, your home, your loved ones, and your dreams.

(Gordon B. Hinckley, "Except the Lord Build the House," *Ensign*, June 1971, 72.)

JULY 10
Practicing Good Manners

But the wisdom that is from above is first pure, then peaceable, gentle, and easy to be intreated, full of mercy and good fruits, without partiality, and without hypocrisy.

JAMES 3:17

See also James 3:18; Mosiah 4:13; 3 Ne. 12:9.

Learn good manners. Practice good manners at home; speak politely and correctly at home. Then, when you go abroad into society, you feel at ease, because you are natural. You do there what you do everywhere, speak and act as a gentleman or a lady should. A Latter-day Saint, who lives according to the rules of his or her religion, is thereby made a gentleman or lady. Such persons cannot be anything else.

(George Q. Cannon, *Gospel Truth: Discourses and Writings of President George Q. Cannon*, ed. Jerreld L. Newquist [Salt Lake City: Deseret Book, 1987], 462.)

JULY 11

Knowing the Will of the Lord

Wherefore, my beloved brethren, reconcile yourselves to the will of God, and not to the will of the devil and the flesh; and remember, after ye are reconciled unto God, that it is only in and through the grace of God that ye are saved.

2 NE. 10:24

See also Alma 32:19; 3 Ne. 6:18; D&C 46:30.

If all our selfish motives, then, and all our personal desires and expediency would be subordinated to a desire to know the will of the Lord, one could have the companionship of heavenly vision. If our problems be too great for human intelligence or too much for human strength, we too, if we are faithful and appeal rightly unto the source of divine power, might have standing by us in our hour of peril or great need an angel of God.

(Harold B. Lee, *The Teachings of Harold B. Lee*, ed. Clyde J. Williams [Salt Lake City: Bookcraft, 1996], 614.)

JULY 12
Honoring One's Mate

Nevertheless neither is the man without the woman, neither the woman without the man, in the Lord.

1 COR. 11:11

See also D&C 132:19–20; 25:14; 1 Pet. 3:7.

I desire with all my heart to honor and respect my husband as my head, ever to live in his confidence and by acting in unison with him retain the place which God has given me by his side.

(Emma Hale Smith, as quoted in Janet Peterson and LaRene Gaunt, *Elect Ladies* [Salt Lake City: Deseret Book, 1990], 17–18.)

JULY 13

Lead People to Forsake Sin

Wherefore, be faithful; stand in the office which I have appointed unto you; succor the weak, lift up the hands which hang down, and strengthen the feeble knees.

D&C 81:5

See also Moro. 6:4; D&C 20:47; 108:7; 121:42.

Nothing is so much calculated to lead people to forsake sin as to take them by the hand, and watch over them with tenderness. When persons manifest the least kindness and love to me, O what power it has over my mind, while the opposite course has a tendency to harrow up all the harsh feelings and depress the human mind.

(Joseph Smith, *Encyclopedia of Joseph Smith's Teachings*, ed. Larry E. Dahl and Donald Q. Cannon [Salt Lake City: Bookcraft, 1997])

JULY 14

Renewing Covenants through the Sacrament

O God, the Eternal Father, we ask thee in the name of thy Son, Jesus Christ, to bless and sanctify this wine to the souls of all those who drink of it, that they may do it in remembrance of the blood of thy Son, which was shed for them; that they may witness unto thee, O God, the Eternal Father, that they do always remember him, that they may have his Spirit to be with them. Amen.

D&C 20:79

See also Matt. 26:26–28; 1 Cor. 11:26–29; 3 Ne.18:7; 20:3; 26:13; Moro. 5:2

Our Heavenly Father has provided a way that we can renew the covenants we made with him at the time of our baptism. Each week we can gather together to partake of the sacrament for that purpose. It is not very likely that during the course of a week, between sacrament meetings, we will get so far off the path of righteousness that we will lose our way. There is always that still, small voice to guide us.

(Boyd K. Packer, *Let Not Your Heart Be Troubled* [Salt Lake City: Bookcraft, 1991], 233.)

JULY 15
Continually Be Optimistic

Therefore, dearly beloved brethren, let us cheerfully do all things that lie in our power; and then may we stand still, with the utmost assurance, to see the salvation of God, and for his arm to be revealed.

D&C 123:17

See also Prov. 15:13; 3 Ne. 1:13; Ether 12:4.

Yet, of all people, we as Latter-day Saints should be the most optimistic and the least pessimistic. For while we know that "peace shall be taken from the earth, and the devil shall have power over his own dominion," we are also assured that "the Lord shall have power over his saints, and shall reign in their midst" (D&C 1:35–36).

(Ezra Taft Benson, *The Teachings of Ezra Taft Benson* [Salt Lake City: Bookcraft, 1988], 401.)

JULY 16
Doing the Will of God

Not every one that saith unto me, Lord, Lord, shall enter into the kingdom of heaven; but he that doeth the will of my Father who is in heaven.

3 NE. 14:21

See also Matt. 7:21; Mark 3:35; Luke 22:42; 1 Jn. 2:15–17; 3 Ne. 6:17–18.

Religion is more than the confession and profession of the lips. . . . Only by doing the will of the Father is the saving grace of the Son obtainable. To assume to speak and act in the name of the Lord without the bestowal of authority, such as the Lord alone can give, is to add sacrilege to hypocrisy. Even miracles wrought will be no vindication of the claims of those who pretend to minister in the ordinances of the gospel while devoid of the authority of the Holy Priesthood.

(James E. Talmage, *Jesus the Christ*, [Salt Lake City: Bookcraft, 1983], 229.)

JULY 17

Don't Be Unfair to Yourself

For all have not every gift given unto them; for there are many gifts, and to every man is given a gift by the Spirit of God.

D&C 46:11

See also 1 Cor. 7:7; 12:4; 1 Ne. 4:6.

One of the great tragedies of life, it seems to me, is when a person classifies himself as someone who has no talents or gifts. When, in disgust or discouragement, we allow ourselves to reach depressive levels of despair because of our demeaning self-appraisal, it is a sad day for us and a sad day in the eyes of God. For us to conclude that we have no gifts when we judge ourselves by stature, intelligence, grade-point average, wealth, power, position, or external appearance is not only unfair but unreasonable.

(Marvin J. Ashton, "There Are Many Gifts," *Ensign*, Nov. 1987, 20–21.)

Therefore, my beloved brethren, be ye stedfast, unmoveable, always abounding in the work of the Lord, forasmuch as ye know that your labour is not in vain in the Lord.

1 COR. 15:58

See also 1 Ne. 1:21; 2 Ne. 31:20; Mosiah 5:15; Hel. 6:1.

"What prompts such devotion on the part of every worker?" the answer can be stated simply: an individual testimony of the gospel of the Lord Jesus Christ, even a heartfelt desire to love the Lord with all one's heart, mind, and soul, and one's neighbor as oneself.

(Thomas S. Monson, *Be Your Best Self* [Salt Lake City: Deseret Book, 1979], 181.)

Keeping the Covenants

I baptize thee, having authority from the Almighty God, as a testimony that ye have entered into a covenant to serve him until you are dead as to the mortal body; and may the Spirit of the Lord be poured out upon you; and may he grant unto you eternal life, through the redemption of Christ, whom he has prepared from the foundation of the world.

MOSIAH 18:13

See also D&C 52:15–16; 132:6–7.

If you keep the covenants and commandments of God, you will have the joy promised by the Savior when he walked upon the earth. You will have "peace in this world, and eternal life in the world to come" (D&C 59:23).

(James E. Faust, *Reach Up for the Light* [Salt Lake City: Deseret Book, 1990], 69.)

JULY 20

Be a Strong Link in Your Own Family Chain

And he shall turn the heart of the fathers to the children, and the heart of the children to their fathers, lest I come and smite the earth with a curse.

MALACHI 4:6

See also 3 Ne. 25:3–6; D&C 38:47–48; 131.

I would hope and pray that in our own families, all of us, that we would have a desire to be a strong link in our own family chain, in our posterity, so that the eternal blessings that are part of the gospel, the blessings of the temple and the eternities, will be taught to our families in such a way that they will go on and on forever to affect many, many people. Be sure that those links are strong in your chain and that you pass the testimony that you have, the devotion that you have to future generations.

(David B. Haight, "Faith, Devotion, and Gratitude," *Ensign*, May 2000, 34.)

JULY 21
Peace and Comfort

Learn of me, and listen to my words; walk in the meekness of my Spirit, and you shall have peace in me.

D&C 19:23

See also Isa. 48:22; John 14:27; James 3:18.

There is no real peace, there is no real happiness in anything in heaven or on the earth, except to those who serve the Lord. In His service there is joy, there is happiness; but they are not to be found anywhere else. In it there are peace and comfort; but when the soul is filled with joy, with peace, and with glory, and is perfectly satisfied therewith a person even then has but little idea of that which is in store for all the faithful.

(Brigham Young, remarks in the Bowery, July 5, 1857, *Journal of Discourses*, 26 vols. [London: Latter-day Saints' Book Depot, 1854–1886], 5:1–2.)

And he said unto them, The sabbath was made for man, and not man for the sabbath.

MARK 2:27

See also Ex. 20:8; Deut. 5:12; Mark 3:4.

In our day, standards for keeping the Sabbath day holy are lowered a little at a time by some individuals until practically anything seems to become acceptable. The sign between the Lord and his covenant people is trampled underfoot as Latter-day Saints skip Sunday meetings to seek recreation at lakes and beaches, in the mountains, at sports arenas, and at theaters. Parking lots at supermarkets and discount stores often are full on Sundays. . . . The people who misuse the Sabbath lose the blessings of spiritual food and growth promised to those who keep this commandment.

(Joseph B. Wirthlin, *Finding Peace in Our Lives* [Salt Lake City: Deseret Book, 1995], 16.)

Righteous Family Traditions

And it came to pass that whosoever would not believe in the tradition of the Lamanites, but believed those records which were brought out of the land of Jerusalem, and also in the tradition of their fathers, which were correct, who believed in the commandments of God and kept them, were called the Nephites, or the people of Nephi, from that time forth.

ALMA 3:11

See also 2 Thes. 2:15; Mosiah 10:12; Alma 9:8.

If we will build righteous traditions in our families, the light of the gospel can grow ever brighter in the lives of our children from generation to generation. We can look forward to that glorious day when we will all be united together as eternal family units to reap the everlasting joy promised by our Eternal Father for His righteous children.

(L. Tom Perry, "Family Traditions," *Ensign*, May 1990, 20.)

JULY 24

Being Valiant

And they were all young men, and they were exceedingly valiant for courage, and also for strength and activity; but behold, this was not all—they were men who were true at all times in whatsoever thing they were entrusted.

ALMA 53:20

See also 2 Sam. 17:10; D&C 76:79.

I will go forward. I will smile at the rage of the tempest, and ride fearlessly and triumphantly across the boisterous ocean of circumstance . . . and 'the testimony of Jesus' will light up a lamp that will guide my vision through the portals of immortality, and communicate to my understanding the glories of the Celestial kingdom.

(Eliza R. Snow, quoted in Janet Peterson and LaRene Gaunt, *Elect Ladies* [Salt Lake City: Deseret Book, 1990], 40.)

JULY 25

Honesty: The Only Policy

Thou shalt not bear false witness against thy neighbour.

Ex. 20:16

See also 2 Ne. 9:34; Alma 27:27; D&C 98:10.

Simple honesty is so remarkable a quality. It is of the very essence of integrity. It demands that we be straightforward, unequivocal, in walking the straight and narrow line of what is right and true. It is so easy to cheat. At times it is so enticing to do so. Better a poor grade than a dishonest act.

(Gordon B. Hinckley, *Teachings of Gordon B. Hinckley* [Salt Lake City: Deseret Book, 1997], 269.)

JULY 26
Life after Death

For as in Adam all die, even so in Christ shall all be made alive.

1 COR. 15:22

See also Prov. 3:5–6; Rev. 14:13; Alma 12:24.

Those who mourn will be consoled as they reaffirm their trust in God. We should not seek "to counsel the Lord, but to take counsel from his hand. For behold, [we] know that he counseleth in wisdom, and in justice, and in great mercy, over all his works" (Jacob 4:10). Neither does the faithful person contend with "an appointed time to man upon earth" (Job 7:1), but he or she begins to understand that triumphs, tribulations, and death are part of life.

(Russell M. Nelson, *The Gateway We Call Death* [Salt Lake City: Deseret Book, 1995], 30–31.)

JULY 27

Calling and Election to Be Made Sure

Wherefore the rather, brethren, give diligence to make your calling and election sure: for if ye do these things, ye shall never fall.

2 PET. 1:10

See also 2 Pet. 1:3–12; D&C 4:6–7; 132:49.

Contend earnestly for the like precious faith with the Apostle Peter, "and add to your faith virtue," knowledge, temperance, patience, godliness, brotherly kindness, charity . . . [A]fter having all these qualifications, he lays this injunction upon the people "to make your calling and election sure." He is emphatic upon this subject—after adding all this virtue, knowledge, etc., "Make your calling and election sure." What is the secret—the starting point? "According as His divine power hath given unto us all things that pertain unto life and godliness." How did he obtain all things? Through the knowledge of Him who hath called him.

(Joseph Smith, *Teachings of the Prophet Joseph Smith*, selected and arranged by Joseph Fielding Smith [Salt Lake City: Deseret Book, 1976], 305.)

JULY 28
Things of the Spirit

But the Comforter, which *is* the Holy Ghost, whom the Father will send in my name, he shall teach you all things, and bring all things to your remembrance, whatsoever I have said unto you.

JOHN 14:26

See also 1 Ne. 4:6; 10:19; 2 Ne. 32:5.

The greatest education and the greatest thrust in our lives ought to be to build upon the things of the Spirit. . . . We cannot ignore keeping the commandments of God. We cannot excuse ourselves or rationalize or justify even the smallest things in our lives that we need to master. We must work to overcome them. We can become the masters of our own destinies by practicing self-discipline, by setting worthy goals that will lead to higher ground so that we can become what our Heavenly Father wants us to become.

(M. Russell Ballard, "Do Things That Make a Difference," *Ensign*, June 1983, 68.)

JULY 29
Quest for Wisdom or Intelligence

The glory of God is intelligence, or, in other words, light and truth.

Light and truth forsake that evil one.

D&C 93:36–37

See also 2 Ne. 28:30; Alma 32:28; 37:35.

This quest for wisdom or intelligence, which the Lord defines as "light and truth" (D&C 93:36), is a glorious challenge. We have been assured by the Author of eternal life that "whatever principle of intelligence we attain unto in this life, it will rise with us in the resurrection. And if a person gains more knowledge and intelligence in this life through his diligence and obedience than another, he will have so much the advantage in the world to come" (D&C 130:18–19).

(Ezra Taft Benson, *The Teachings of Ezra Taft Benson* [Salt Lake City: Bookcraft, 1988], 302.)

What Is the Price of Happiness?

And it came to pass that I beheld a tree, whose fruit was desirable to make one happy.

1 Ne. 8:10

See also 2 Ne. 2:13; Mosiah 2:41; Alma 27:18.

What is the price of happiness? One might be surprised at the simplicity of the answer.

The treasure house of happiness is unlocked to those who live the gospel of Jesus Christ in its purity and simplicity. Like a mariner without stars, like a traveler without a compass, is the person who moves along through life without a plan. The assurance of supreme happiness, the certainty of a successful life here and of exaltation and eternal life hereafter, come to those who plan to live their lives in complete harmony with the gospel of Jesus Christ—and then consistently follow the course they have set.

(Spencer W. Kimball, *The Miracle of Forgiveness* [Salt Lake City: Bookcraft, 1969] 259.)

Hearken and hear, O ye inhabitants of the earth. Listen, ye elders of my church together, and hear the voice of the Lord; for he calleth upon all men, and he commandeth all men everywhere to repent.

D&C 133:16

See also Acts 2:38; 17:30; 2 Ne. 9:23.

The final prophet to speak in that era, a counterpart to Moroni, was Ether, who "did cry from the morning, even until the going down of the sun, exhorting the people to believe in God unto repentance lest they should be destroyed, saying unto them that by faith all things are fulfilled" (Ether 12:3).

(Jeffrey R. Holland, *Christ and the New Covenant: The Messianic Message of the Book of Mormon* [Salt Lake City: Deseret Book, 1997], 327–328.)

AUGUST

And this shall ye always observe to do,
even as I have done.

—3 Nephi 18:6

AUGUST 1

Preparing to Meet Our Maker

I tell you these things because of your prayers;
wherefore, treasure up wisdom in your bosoms, lest the
wickedness of men reveal these things unto you by their
wickedness, in a manner which shall speak in your ears
with a voice louder than that which shall shake the
earth; but if ye are prepared ye shall not fear.

D&C 38:30

See also Alma 5:29; 32:6; 42:26.

We should each live so when that time comes we
will be prepared to meet our maker and have him say
to us, "Well done my good and faithful servant."

(Howard W. Hunter, *The Teachings of Howard W. Hunter*, ed.
Clyde J. Williams [Salt Lake City: Bookcraft, 1997], 15.)

AUGUST 2
Seeking a Testimony

And this is life eternal, that they might know thee the only true God, and Jesus Christ, whom thou hast sent.

JOHN 17:3

See also Mosiah 18:9; D&C 9:8; JS–H 1:26.

Seek for a testimony, as you would, my dear sisters, for a diamond concealed. If someone told you by digging long enough in a certain spot you would find a diamond of unmeasured wealth, do you think you would begrudge time or strength, or means spent to obtain that treasure? Then I will tell you that if you will dig in the depths of your own hearts you will find, with the aid of the Spirit of the Lord, the pearl of great price, the testimony of the truth of this work.

(Zina D. H. Young, quoted in Janet Peterson and LaRene Gaunt, *Elect Ladies* [Salt Lake City: Deseret Book, 1990], 58.)

AUGUST 3

We Live in Troubled Times

When thou art in tribulation, and all these things are come upon thee, even in the latter days, if thou turn to the Lord thy God, and shalt be obedient unto his voice;

(For the Lord thy God is a merciful God;) he will not forsake thee, neither destroy thee, nor forget the covenant of thy fathers which he sware unto them.

DEUT. 4:30–31

See also 2 Cor. 1:3–7; D&C 112:12–14.

We live in troubled times—very troubled times. We hope, we pray, for better days. But that is not to be. The prophecies tell us that. We will not as a people, as families, or as individuals be exempt from the trials to come. No one will be spared the trials common to home and family, work, disappointment, grief, health, aging, ultimately death.

(Boyd K. Packer, "The Cloven Tongues of Fire," *Ensign,* May 2000, 7.)

AUGUST 4
Enduring Patiently

Now when our hearts were depressed, and we were about to turn back, behold, the Lord comforted us, and said: Go amongst thy brethren, the Lamanites, and bear with patience thine afflictions, and I will give unto you success.

ALMA 26:27

See also James 5:8; 2 Ne. 31:20; D&C 101:38.

Patient endurance is to be distinguished from merely being 'acted upon.' Endurance is more than pacing up and down within the cell of our circumstance; it is not only acceptance of the things allotted to us, it is to 'act for ourselves' by magnifying what is allotted to us (see Alma 29:3, 6).

(Neal A. Maxwell, "Endure It Well," *Ensign*, May 1990, 34.)

AUGUST 5
Living for the Good of Others

He that findeth his life shall lose it: and he that loseth his life for my sake shall find it.

MATT. 10:39

See also Rom. 8:17–18; Philip. 3:8; 1 Ne. 17:50.

Specifically stated, this law is, "We live our lives most completely when we strive to make the world better and happier." The law of pure nature, survival of the fittest, is self-preservation at the sacrifice of all else; but in contrast to this law of true spiritual life is, "Deny self for the good of others."

(David O. McKay, *The Improvement Era*, Oct. 1962, 700–701.)

AUGUST 6

Friendship: A Gospel Principle

A man that hath friends must shew himself friendly: and there is a friend that sticketh closer than a brother.

Prov. 18:24

See also James 2:23; D&C 93:45; 121:9.

Like so much of what is worthwhile in life, our needs for friendship are often best met in the home. If our children feel friendship within the family, with each other, and with parents, they will not be desperate for acceptance outside the family. I think one of life's most satisfying accomplishments for my wife and me is to have lived long enough to see our children become good friends.

(Marlin K. Jensen, "Friendship: A Gospel Principle," *Ensign*, May 1999, 64.)

AUGUST 7
Powerful Ideas

And the King shall answer and say unto them, Verily I say unto you, Inasmuch as ye have done it unto one of the least of these my brethren, ye have done it unto me.

MATT. 25:40

See also Matt. 22:36–40; D&C 59:6.

When we understand our relationship to God, we also understand our relationship to one another. All men and women on this earth are the offspring of God, spirit brothers and sisters. What a powerful idea! No wonder God's Only Begotten Son commanded us to love one another. If only we could do so! What a different world it would be if brotherly and sisterly love and unselfish assistance could transcend all boundaries of nation, creed, and color. Such love would not erase all differences of opinion and action, but it would encourage each of us to focus our opposition on actions rather than actors.

(Dallin H. Oaks, "Powerful Ideas," *Ensign*, Nov. 1995, 25.)

AUGUST 8

Reading the Scriptures

Yea, and they had waxed strong in the knowledge of the truth; for they were men of a sound understanding and they had searched the scriptures diligently, that they might know the word of God.

ALMA 17:2

See also John 5:39; 2 Tim. 3:15; D&C 11:22.

I am grateful for emphasis on reading the scriptures. I hope that for you this will become something far more enjoyable than a duty; that, rather, it will become a love affair with the word of God. I promise you that as you read, your minds will be enlightened and your spirits will be lifted. At first it may seem tedious, but that will change into a wondrous experience with thoughts and words of things divine.

(Gordon B. Hinckley, "The Light within You," *Ensign*, May 1995, 99.)

AUGUST 9

Building Our Faith

So then faith cometh by hearing, and hearing by
the word of God.

ROM. 10:17

See also Heb. 11:6; Enos 1:11; Moro. 7:33.

I have come to understand how useless it is to
dwell on the *why*s, *what if*s, and *if only*s for which
there likely will be given no answers in mortality. To
receive the Lord's comfort, we must exercise faith.
The questions Why me? Why our family? Why now?
are usually unanswerable questions. These questions
detract from our spirituality and can destroy our
faith. We need to spend our time and energy building
our faith by turning to the Lord and asking for
strength to overcome the pains and trials of this world
and to endure to the end for greater understanding.

(Robert D. Hales, "Healing Soul and Body," *Ensign*, Nov.
1998, 14.)

AUGUST 10
Saviors on Mount Zion

For they were set to be a light unto the world, and to be the saviors of men; And inasmuch as they are not the saviors of men, they are as salt that has lost its savor, and is thenceforth good for nothing but to be cast out and trodden under foot of men.

D&C 103:9–10

See also D&C 101:39–40; 3 Ne. 12:13.

God is looking upon us, and has called us to be saviors upon Mount Zion. And what does a savior mean? It means a person who saves somebody. Jesus went and preached to the spirits in prison; and he was a savior to that people. When he came to atone for the sins of the world, he was a savior, was he not? . . . Would we be saviors if we did not save somebody? I think not. Could we save anyone if we did not build temples? No, we could not; for God would not accept our offerings and sacrifices. Then we came here to be saviors on Mount Zion, and the kingdom is to be the Lord's.

(John Taylor, *Journal of Discourses*, 26 vols. [London: Latter-day Saints' Book Depot, 1854–1886], 22:308.)

AUGUST 11

Self-Esteem as the Heart of Our Growth

For in him we live, and move, and have our being; as certain also of your own poets have said, For we are also his offspring.

Forasmuch then as we are the offspring of God, we ought not to think that the Godhead is like unto gold, or silver, or stone, graven by art and man's device.

ACTS 17:28–29

See also Rom. 8:16; D&C 84:38.

Self-esteem goes to the very heart of our personal growth and accomplishment. Self-esteem is the glue that holds together our self-reliance, our self-control, our self-approval or disapproval, and keeps all self-defense mechanisms secure. It is a protection against excessive self-deception, self-distrust, self-reproach, and plain, old-fashioned selfishness.

(James E. Faust, *Reach Up for the Light* [Salt Lake City: Deseret Book, 1990], 31.)

AUGUST 12

Feasting at the Table of the Lord

And it came to pass, that, as Jesus sat at meat in his house, many publicans and sinners sat also together with Jesus and his disciples: for there were many, and they followed him.

MARK 2:15

See also John 8:12; 1 Cor. 10:4; 2 Ne. 31:10.

Just as food satisfies our physical hunger, we can partake with satisfaction and delight in all the Father has for us as we, living like his Son, feast at the table of the Lord.

(Michaelene P. Grassli, "Follow Him," *Ensign*, Nov. 1989, 92.)

AUGUST 13
Sometimes We Need Chastening

Verily, thus saith the Lord unto you whom I love, and whom I love I also chasten that their sins may be forgiven, for with the chastisement I prepare a way for their deliverance in all things out of temptation, and I have loved you—

Wherefore, ye must needs be chastened and stand rebuked before my face.

D&C 95:1–2

See also Heb. 12:5–11; Hel. 12:2–3; D&C 1:27.

Sometimes we need chastening. It's an interesting thing that sometimes it takes calamity to drive us together. It's a terrifying thing to think that that's necessary, but the Lord said through one of His prophets that sometimes we have to have the chastening hand of the Almighty before we will wake up and humble ourselves to do the thing that He has asked us to do (see Hel. 12:3–6).

(Harold B. Lee, *The Teachings of Harold B. Lee*, ed. Clyde J. Williams [Salt Lake City: Bookcraft, 1996], 191.)

AUGUST 14
Commitment to Excellence

Wherefore, be not weary in well-doing, for ye are laying the foundation of a great work. And out of small things proceedeth that which is great.

D&C 64:33

See also 1 Cor. 12:31; Ether 12:11.

Excellence comes because it is achieved, and it cannot be achieved except by strict discipline and definiteness of purpose.

(Howard W. Hunter, *The Teachings of Howard W. Hunter*, ed. Clyde J. Williams [Salt Lake City: Bookcraft, 1997], 61.)

AUGUST 15

Great Things Depend on Individual Exertion

Thou hast commanded us to keep thy precepts diligently.

Ps. 119:4

See also Alma 32:42; Moro. 9:6; D&C 18:8.

Let the Saints remember that great things depend on their individual exertion, and that they are called to be co-workers with us and the Holy Spirit in accomplishing the great work of the last days; and in consideration of the extent, the blessings and glories of the same, let every selfish feeling be not only buried, but annihilated; and let love to God and man predominate, and reign triumphant in every mind, that their hearts may become like unto Enoch's of old, and comprehend all things, present, past and future, and come behind in no gift, waiting for the coming of the Lord Jesus Christ.

(Joseph Smith Jr., *Teachings of the Prophet Joseph Smith*, sel. Joseph Fielding Smith [Salt Lake City: Deseret Book, 1976], 178.)

AUGUST 16
Having a Reverent Attitude

The fear of the Lord is the instruction of wisdom; and before honour is humility.

PROV. 15:33

See also 1 Sam. 12:24; Ps. 2:11; 112:1.

Reverence is an attitude of deepest love and respect for Heavenly Father and our Lord, Jesus Christ. It is not enough to behave reverently; we must feel it in our hearts. Reverent behavior without a reverent attitude is empty of meaning if it is performed only for the praises of men.

(L. Tom Perry, "Reverence," *Friend*, Jan. 1992, inside front cover.)

AUGUST 17
Humility Does Not Mean Weakness

Nevertheless they did fast and pray oft, and did wax stronger and stronger in their humility, and firmer and firmer in the faith of Christ, unto the filling their souls with joy and consolation, yea, even to the purifying and the sanctification of their hearts, which sanctification cometh because of their yielding their hearts unto God.

HEL. 3:35

See also James 4:10; Alma 32:16; Ether 12:27.

The Lord has made it very clear that no man can assist with this work unless he is humble and full of love (see D&C 12:8). But humility does not mean timidity. Humility does not mean fear. Humility does not mean weakness. You can be humble and still be courageous. You can be humble and still be vigorous and strong and fearless.

(Ezra Taft Benson, *The Teachings of Ezra Taft Benson* [Salt Lake City: Bookcraft, 1988], 199.)

AUGUST 18
Sharing the Gospel

And now, behold, I say unto you, that the thing which will be of the most worth unto you will be to declare repentance unto this people, that you may bring souls unto me, that you may rest with them in the kingdom of my Father. Amen.

D&C 15:6

See also Morm. 9:22; D&C 33:8–11; 123:12.

The First Presidency has said that one of the threefold missions of the Church is to proclaim the gospel. If we accept this mission, we should be willing to center our efforts on bringing souls unto the Lord on condition of repentance. . . . There are many ways to share the gospel.... *Step one:* Prayerfully *set a date.* . . . *Step two:* Prayerfully choose a friend. . . . *Step three:* Share your date and your plans with your bishopric. . . . *Step four:* With the help of the Spirit, invite your nonmember friend to hear the missionary discussions.

(M. Russell Ballard, "We Proclaim the Gospel," *Ensign*, Nov. 1986, 31.)

AUGUST 19
Believe in Jesus Christ

And he shall be called Jesus Christ, the Son of God, the Father of heaven and earth, the Creator of all things from the beginning; and his mother shall be called Mary.

MOSIAH 3:8

See also 2 Ne. 31:16; 3 Ne. 18:24; D&C 93:9.

Believe in Jesus Christ, the Savior and Redeemer of the world. It is He who stands at the head of this Church to which you belong. This Church is not mine. It belongs to the Lord Jesus Christ. It bears His holy name. He stands at the head of this great work. He stands to assist us with our problems. He stands to bless us in our time of need.

(Gordon B. Hinckley, *Teachings of Gordon B. Hinckley* [Salt Lake City: Deseret Book, 1997], 199.)

AUGUST 20

Searching for Truth

And that wicked one cometh and taketh away light and truth, through disobedience, from the children of men, and because of the tradition of their fathers.

D&C 93:39

See also Ps. 119:142; Ether 4:12; D&C 93:24, 28.

Fill your mind with truth. I'd like to suggest that when we search for truth, we search among those books and in those places where truth is most likely to be found. I've often referred to a simple couplet: "You do not find truth groveling through error. You find truth by searching the holy word of God." There are those who for direction and inspiration turn to the philosophies of man. There a smattering of truth may be found, but not the entire spectrum.

(Thomas S. Monson, *Be Your Best Self* [Salt Lake City: Deseret Book, 1979], 169.)

AUGUST 21
What We Get Depends on What We Seek

Whosoever shall seek to save his life shall lose it; and whosoever shall lose his life shall preserve it.

LUKE 17:33

See also John 5:30; Acts 17:27; 1 Cor. 14:12.

Someone has said that what we get depends on what we seek. Persons who attend Church solely in order to *get* something of a temporal nature may be disappointed. The Apostle Paul wrote disparagingly of persons who "serve not our Lord Jesus Christ, but their own belly" (Rom. 16:18). Persons who attend Church in order to *give* to their fellowmen and *serve* the Lord will rarely be disappointed. The Savior promised that "he that loseth his life for my sake shall find it" (Matt. 10:39).

(Dallin H. Oaks, "The Gospel in Our Lives," *Ensign*, May 2002, 33.)

AUGUST 22
Putting First Things First

❧

Wherefore, be not weary in well-doing, for ye are laying the foundation of a great work. And out of small things proceedeth that which is great.

D&C 64:33

See also D&C 58:27; 103:36; 107:99–100.

How do I use my discretionary time? Is some of it consistently applied to my highest priorities? Is there anything I know I should not be doing? If so, I will repent and stop it now. In a quiet moment write down your responses. Analyze them. Make any necessary adjustments. Put first things first.

(Richard G. Scott, "First Things First," *Ensign*, May 2001, 9.)

AUGUST 23

A Harmonizing Book

And gave him power from on high, by the means which were before prepared, to translate the Book of Mormon; ...Which was given by inspiration, and is confirmed to others by the ministering of angels, and is declared unto the world by them—Proving to the world that the holy scriptures are true, and that God does inspire men and call them to his holy work in this age and generation, as well as in generations of old.

D&C 20:8–11

See also Isa. 29:4; Ezek. 37:19; John 10:16.

There is not a doctrine taught in it that does not harmonize with the teachings of Jesus Christ. There is not one single expression in the Book of Mormon that would wound in the slightest degree the sensitiveness of any individual. There is not a thing in it but what is for the benefit and uplift of mankind. It is in every way a true witness for God, and it sustains the Bible, and is in harmony with the Bible.

(Heber J. Grant, *Gospel Standards: Selections from the Sermons and Writings of Heber J. Grant*, comp. G. Homer Durham [Salt Lake City: Improvement Era, 1981], 27.)

AUGUST 24

Feeling the Love of the Lord

Grace be with you, mercy, and peace, from God the Father, and from the Lord Jesus Christ, the Son of the Father, in truth and love.

2 Jn. 1:3

See also Ps. 86:15; Tim. 1:16; D&C 121:45.

If I could have one thing happen for every woman in this Church, it would be that they would feel the love of the Lord in their lives.

(Bonnie D. Parkin, "Feel the Love of the Lord," *Ensign*, May 2002, 84.)

AUGUST 25
Pure Rest of a Clear Conscience

Unto the pure all things are pure: but unto them that are defiled and unbelieving is nothing pure; but even their mind and conscience is defiled.

TITUS 1:15

See also Moro. 7:15–19; D&C 84:45–47.

The first condition of happiness is a clear conscience. . . . Uprightness of character, honesty in dealing with your fellow men, honor bright, your word as good as your bond, then when your head touches your pillow at night, and you contemplate your actions during the day, you sleep with a good conscience.

(David O. McKay, *Gospel Ideals: Selections from the Discourses of David O. McKay* [Salt Lake City: Improvement Era, 1953], 498.)

AUGUST 26
Understanding the Truth

Give me understanding, and I shall keep thy law;
yea, I shall observe it with my whole heart.

Ps. 119:34

See also Prov. 3:13; Alma 13:28; D&C 50:10–12.

But let every man seek earnestly to understand
the truth and teach his children to become familiar
with those truths of heaven that have been restored to
the earth in the Latter-days.

(Joseph F. Smith, *Gospel Doctrine: Selections from the Sermons
and Writings of Joseph F. Smith*, comp. John A. Widtsoe [Salt Lake
City: Deseret Book, 1939], 5.)

AUGUST 27

Submit to the Will of Our Heavenly Father

For whosoever shall do the will of my Father which is in heaven, the same is my brother, and sister, and mother.

MATT. 12:50

See also John 4:34; 3 Ne. 1:14; 27:13.

It won't be enough for them simply to listen to the word of God. They must choose to keep commandments because they feel at least a beginning desire to know the will of our Heavenly Father and submit to it. That feeling of surrender is not likely to come unless they experience some feeling of being loved and some value in their being meek and lowly of heart.

(Henry B. Eyring, "To Touch a Life with Faith," *Ensign,* Nov. 1995, 37.)

AUGUST 28
Being a Covenant People

But behold, there shall be many—at that day when I shall proceed to do a marvelous work among them, that I may remember my covenants which I have made unto the children of men, that I may set my hand again the second time to recover my people, which are of the house of Israel.

2 NE. 29:1

See also 1 Ne. 17:40; 2 Ne. 9:1–2; D&C 110:12.

If there is a distinguishing feature about members of the Church, it is that we make covenants. That involves staying the course, being constant and steadfast. It means keeping the faith and being faithful to the end despite success or failure, doubt or discouragement. It is drawing near to the Lord with all our hearts. It is doing whatever we promise to do with all our might—even when we might not feel like it.

(F. Burton Howard, "Commitment," *Ensign*, May 1996, 27.)

AUGUST 29

Obedience: Our Quest

If ye love me, keep my commandments.
JOHN 14:15

See also 1 Ne. 22:31; D&C 130:19–21.

Every son and daughter of God is expected to obey with a willing heart every word which the Lord has spoken, and which he will in the future speak to us. It is expected that we hearken to the revelations of his will, and adhere to them, cleave to them with all our might; for this is salvation, and any thing short of this clips the salvation and the glory of the Saints.

(Brigham Young, *Discourses of Brigham Young*, sel. John A. Widtsoe [Salt Lake City: Deseret Book, 1954], 220.)

AUGUST 30
Avoiding Temptation

And why should I yield to sin, because of my flesh? Yea, why should I give way to temptations, that the evil one have place in my heart to destroy my peace and afflict my soul? Why am I angry because of mine enemy?

2 NE. 4:27

See also JST–Matt. 6:14; 3 Ne. 18:18; Morm. 9:28.

A personal testimony of the Savior and his atonement can help us avoid temptation. Strive to build a personal testimony of Jesus Christ and the atonement. . . . When temptations come, as they surely will, an understanding of the Savior's agony in Gethsemane and his eventual death on the cross will be a reminder to you to avoid any activity that would cause the Savior more pain.

(Howard W. Hunter, *The Teachings of Howard W. Hunter*, ed. Clyde J. Williams [Salt Lake City: Bookcraft, 1997], 31.)

And wo be unto him that will not hearken unto the words of Jesus, and also to them whom he hath chosen and sent among them; for whoso receiveth not the words of Jesus and the words of those whom he hath sent receiveth not him; and therefore he will not receive them at the last day.

3 NE. 28:34

See also 2 Chr. 20:20; Matt. 10:40; D&C 107:22.

If we do not sustain the living prophet, whoever he may be, we die spiritually. Ironically, some have died spiritually by exclusively following prophets who have long been dead. Others equivocate in their support of living prophets, trying to lift themselves up by putting down the living prophets, however subtly.

(James E. Faust, *Reach Up for the Light* [Salt Lake City: Deseret Book, 1990], 111.)

 EPTEMBER

*Blessed are ye if ye shall give heed unto
the words of these twelve . . .*

—3 Nephi 12:1

SEPTEMBER 1

*Missionary Work—Finding
and Friendshipping*

For there are many yet on the earth among all
sects, parties, and denominations, who are blinded by
the subtle craftiness of men, whereby they lie in wait
to deceive, and who are only kept from the truth
because they know not where to find it.

D&C 123:12

See also Alma 29:9–10; D&C 33:8–11.

You will learn the importance of friendshipping
and fellowshipping. Now is the time to practice these
principles, to reach out with appreciation and kindness to others. Many a young man has come into this
Church because of the friendship of a high school
associate. I earnestly hope that no boy within the
sound of my voice will ever do anything to prejudice
an associate against the Church or its people.

(Gordon B. Hinckley, *Teachings of Gordon B. Hinckley* [Salt
Lake City: Deseret Book, 1997], 222.)

SEPTEMBER 2
Learning Self-Mastery

Then said Jesus unto his disciples, If any man will come after me, let him deny himself, and take up his cross, and follow me.

MATT. 16:24

See also 1 Cor. 9:25; 1 Pet. 3:10; 2 Ne. 4:16–35.

We are here to learn self–mastery. By learning to govern our natures, our appetites and passions, we draw closer to the divine nature of God, thereby fulfilling the mandate of the Master to "be . . . perfect, even as [our] Father which is in heaven is perfect" (Matt. 5:48).

(Ezra Taft Benson, *Come unto Christ* [Salt Lake City: Deseret Book, 1983], 74.)

SEPTEMBER 3
Instilling Self-Confidence

Let thy bowels also be full of charity towards all men, and to the household of faith, and let virtue garnish thy thoughts unceasingly; then shall thy confidence wax strong in the presence of God; and the doctrine of the priesthood shall distil upon thy soul as the dews from heaven.

D&C 121:45

See also Prov. 3:26; 1 Ne. 3:7.

The teacher not only shapes the expectations and ambitions of her pupils, but she also influences their attitudes toward their future and themselves. If she is unskilled, she leaves scars on the lives of youth, cuts deeply into their self-esteem, and distorts their image of themselves as human beings. But if she loves her students and has high expectations of them, their self-confidence will grow, their capabilities will develop, and their future will be assured.

(Thomas S. Monson, *Pathways to Perfection* [Salt Lake City: Deseret Book, 1973], 173.)

SEPTEMBER 4

Be Careful in Judging

Judge not, that ye be not judged.

MATT. 7:1

See also JST–Matt. 2–5; John 7:24; 8:15–16.

Don't be too anxious to call yourself a failure or to judge others as failures. When all accounts are settled, you will find that no effort to teach righteousness is ever completely lost. Nothing you do in the way of trying to convey the gospel of Jesus Christ is ever futile.

(Boyd K. Packer, *Teach Ye Diligently* [Salt Lake City: Deseret Book, 1975], 339.)

SEPTEMBER 5
Duty of Every Saint

And the members shall manifest before the church, and also before the elders, by a godly walk and conversation, that they are worthy of it, that there may be works and faith agreeable to the holy scriptures—walking in holiness before the Lord.

D&C 20:69

See also Eccl. 12:13; Luke 17:10; Mosiah 1:17.

It is a duty which every saint ought to render to his brethren freely—to always love them, and ever succor them. To be justified before God we must love one another: we must overcome evil; we must visit the fatherless and the widow in their affliction, and we must keep ourselves unspotted from the world: for such virtues flow from the great fountain of pure religion.

(Joseph Smith, *History of The Church of Jesus Christ of Latter-day Saints*, 7 vols., ed. B. H. Roberts [Salt Lake City: The Church of Jesus Christ of Latter-day Saints, 1932–1951], 2:229.)

SEPTEMBER 6
The Spirit of the Lord

Having been visited by the Spirit of God; having conversed with angels, and having been spoken unto by the voice of the Lord; and having the spirit of prophecy, and the spirit of revelation, and also many gifts, the gift of speaking with tongues, and the gift of preaching, and the gift of the Holy Ghost, and the gift of translation.

ALMA 9:21

See also Acts 13:2; 13:9; 2 Ne. 32:5.

The work which we have come into this life to perform cannot be done to the glory of God or to the satisfaction of ourselves merely by our own natural intelligence. We are dependent upon the Spirit of the Lord. . . . It is the privilege of Latter-day Saints, when they get into difficulties, to have supernatural power of God, and in faith, day by day, to secure from the circumstances which may surround us that which will be beneficial and advance us in the principles of holiness and sanctification, that we may as far as possible be like our Father.

(Lorenzo Snow, in Conference Report, Oct. 6, 1898, 109.)

SEPTEMBER 7

Teaching is the Greatest Call

And again, inasmuch as parents have children in Zion, or in any of her stakes which are organized, that teach them not to understand the doctrine of repentance, faith in Christ the Son of the living God, and of baptism and the gift of the Holy Ghost by the laying on of the hands, when eight years old, the sin be upon the heads of the parents. . . .

And they shall also teach their children to pray, and to walk uprightly before the Lord.

D&C 68:25, 28

See also Mosiah 23:14; Alma 17:2–3; D&C 42:14.

I believe there is no greater call in the Church than to be an effective teacher. Effective teaching by the Spirit can stir the souls of men with a desire to live the principles of the gospel of Jesus Christ more completely.

(M. Russell Ballard, "Teaching—No Greater Call," *Ensign*, May 1983, 68.)

SEPTEMBER 8
Kinder Relationships

A new commandment I give unto you, That ye love one another; as I have loved you, that ye also love one another.

By this shall all men know that ye are my disciples, if ye have love one to another.

JOHN 13:34–35

See also Rom. 8:16; 1 Jn. 5:2.

We should try to be more constant and unfailing, more longsuffering and kind, less envious and puffed up in our relationships with others. As Christ lived so should we live, and as Christ loved so should we love.

(Jeffrey R. Holland, *Christ and the New Covenant: The Messianic Message of the Book of Mormon* [Salt Lake City: Deseret Book, 1997], 336–337.)

SEPTEMBER 9

Magnifying Our Calling

And we did magnify our office unto the Lord, taking upon us the responsibility, answering the sins of the people upon our own heads if we did not teach them the word of God with all diligence.

JACOB 1:19

See also Alma 17:2–3; D&C 81:5; 84:33.

The Prophet Joseph was often asked, "Brother Joseph, what do you mean by magnifying a calling?" Joseph replied: "It means to build it up in dignity and importance, to make it honorable and commendable in the eyes of all men, to enlarge and strengthen it, to let the light of heaven shine through it to the view of other men. And how does one magnify a calling? Simply by performing the service that pertains to it."

(Thomas S. Monson, *Pathways to Perfection* [Salt Lake City: Deseret Book, 1973], 146.)

And we are willing to enter into a covenant with our God to do his will, and to be obedient to his commandments in all things that he shall command us, all the remainder of our days.

MOSIAH 5:5

See also D&C 4:2; 64:33; 107:99.

While we are taught to develop our talents and provide for our families, nevertheless we must be careful not to let the pursuit of our career path divert us from the gospel path. We must be "true to the truth" and stay on the "strait and narrow path which leads to eternal life" (2 Nephi 31:18). Remember Alma's counsel to his son Corianton: "Suffer not yourself to be led away by any vain or foolish thing" (Alma 39:11).

(Joseph B. Wirthlin, "True to the Truth," *Ensign*, May 1997, 15.)

SEPTEMBER 11
Making God the Prime Object of Our Love

And thou shalt love the Lord thy God with all thine heart, and with all thy soul, and with all thy might.

DEUT. 6:5

See also 1 Jn. 4:19; D&C 20:19; 42:29.

God is the prime object of our love. It is not enough for us to acknowledge the Lord as supreme and refrain from worshiping idols; we should love the Lord with all our heart, might, mind, and strength. We should honor him and follow him into the work of eternal life. What joy he has in the righteousness of his children!

(Spencer W. Kimball, *The Teachings of Spencer W. Kimball*, ed. Edward L. Kimball [Salt Lake City: Bookcraft, 1982], 243.)

SEPTEMBER 12
Joyfully Testifying

But none of these things move me, neither count I my life dear unto myself, so that I might finish my course with joy, and the ministry, which I have received of the Lord Jesus, to testify the gospel of the grace of God.

ACTS 20:24

See also John 15:26; 2 Ne. 27:12; D&C 20:26.

I am grateful beyond expression that it has fallen to my lot, in humility, but with gratitude and thanksgiving to God, to lift up my voice and testify that God lives, that Jesus is the Christ, the Son of the living God. . . . I have never found one thing that has in the slightest degree affected my faith or caused me to have any doubts regarding the divinity of the work in which we as Latter-day Saints are engaged.

(Heber J. Grant, *Gospel Standards: Selections from the Sermons and Writings of Heber J. Grant*, comp. G. Homer Durham [Salt Lake City: Improvement Era, 1981], 203.)

SEPTEMBER 13
Never Faltering in Faith

Now faith is the substance of things hoped for,
the evidence of things not seen.

HEB. 11:1

See also Moro. 7:33, 42; 10:4–5; A of F 1:4.

From the day I received the sweet testimony of
the Spirit, when grasping the precious Book of
Mormon in my hands to my breast, I have never
doubted nor faltered in my faith. I know this is the
Church and Kingdom of God, and I rejoice in putting
my testimony before the daughters of Zion, that their
faith may be strengthened, and that the good work
may roll on.

(Zina D. H. Young, quoted in Janet Peterson and LaRene
Gaunt, *Elect Ladies* [Salt Lake City: Deseret Book, 1990], 58.)

SEPTEMBER 14
Beauty of Character

Let me be weighed in an even balance, that God may know mine integrity.

JOB 31:6

See also Esther 2:7; Alma 53:20; D&C 124:15.

I am grateful for the opportunity of serving, . . . particularly in Relief Society where during most of my mature life I have worked so happily and contentedly with its thousands of members. I have visited in their homes, slept in their beds, and eaten at their tables and have thus learned of their beauty of character, their unselfishness, their understanding hearts, their faithfulness, and their sacrifices. I honor beyond my power of expression this great sisterhood of service.

(Amy Brown Lyman, quoted in Janet Peterson and LaRene Gaunt, *Elect Ladies* [Salt Lake City: Deseret Book, 1990], 142.)

SEPTEMBER 15

Reinforcing Meekness and Humility

Preach unto them repentance, and faith on the Lord Jesus Christ; teach them to humble themselves and to be meek and lowly in heart; teach them to withstand every temptation of the devil, with their faith on the Lord Jesus Christ.

ALMA 37:33

See also Alma 37:34; 38:14; D&C 32:1; 112:10.

Faith in Christ and hope in his promises of resurrected, eternal life can come only to the meek and lowly in heart. Such promises, in turn, reinforce meekness and lowliness of heart in that believer. Only thorough disciples of Christ, living as meekly as he lived and humbling themselves as he humbled himself, can declare uncompromised faith in Christ and have genuine hope in the Resurrection. These then, and only these, come to understand true charity—the pure love of Christ.

(Jeffrey R. Holland, *Christ and the New Covenant: The Messianic Message of the Book of Mormon* [Salt Lake City: Deseret Book, 1997], 335.)

SEPTEMBER 16

Repeating Righteous Patterns

Howbeit for this cause I obtained mercy, that in me first Jesus Christ might shew forth all long-suffering, for a pattern to them which should hereafter believe on him to life everlasting.

1 TIM. 1:16

See also Heb. 9:23; D&C 52:19; Moses 6:46.

In every imaginable setting from ancient times to modern days, we see this pattern repeated—faith in the Lord Jesus Christ, repentance, baptism, the gift of the Holy Ghost.

(Janette Hales Beckham, "A Pattern of Righteousness," *Ensign*, May 1991, 83.)

SEPTEMBER 17

The Superior Man

Beloved, now are we the sons of God, and it doth not yet appear what we shall be: but we know that, when he shall appear, we shall be like him; for we shall see him as he is.

1 Jn. 3:2

See also Acts 17:29; D&C 32:37; 76:58.

The superior man is spiritual. He exemplifies simplicity. He abhors being conspicuous. He is dedicated to service. Superior people are never bitter. Pessimism is the philosophy of vulgarity. The superior person is clean. His fellowship is refreshing. He is above his pleasures. . . . A superior man is gentle. . . . Superior men are humble-minded, or teachable, and they learn from passersby. The superior man is one with whom familiarity does not breed contempt. The superior man lasts; he wears well.

(Harold B. Lee, "Memorial Service for President Dwight D. Eisenhower, March 1969," *The Teachings of Harold B. Lee,* 607.)

SEPTEMBER 18
Charity Never Faileth

For charity never faileth. Wherefore, cleave unto charity, which is the greatest of all, for all things must fail—

But charity is the pure love of Christ, and it endureth forever; and whoso is found possessed of it at the last day, it shall be well with him.

MORO. 7:46–47

See also Isa. 1:17; 1 Pet. 4:8; 1 Cor. 13:8.

Even as a sister do I love and esteem you—those who feel for me, who administer to my wants, who always seek to cheer and comfort me—they to me are sisters indeed, and in the truest sense of the word; the kindness, the sympathy and cordiality, with which I have been treated by you, constrains me to love you, as well as the rest of the band of sisters, with which I have (very fortunately) become associated and I would to heaven that the same benevolent and generous principles which exist in the bosoms of those of whom I now speak also had an existence in every female who helps to form this vast community.

(Emmeline B. Wells, quoted in Janet Peterson and LaRene Gaunt, *Elect Ladies* [Salt Lake City: Deseret Book, 1990], 94.)

SEPTEMBER 19

Conversion and Happiness

If ye love me, keep my commandments.
JOHN 14:15

See also Mosiah 2:41; 5:2; 4 Ne. 1:15–16.

To be converted, you must remember to apply diligently in your life the key words "a love of God, with a fixed and controlling determination to keep his commandments" (Marion G. Romney, "According to the Covenants," *Ensign*, Nov. 1975). Your happiness now and forever is conditioned on your degree of conversion and the transformation that it brings to your life.

(Richard G. Scott, "Full Conversion Brings Happiness," *Ensign*, May 2002, 25.)

SEPTEMBER 20

Fasting Brings Us in Tune with God

And on this day thou shalt do none other thing, only let thy food be prepared with singleness of heart that thy fasting may be perfect, or, in other words, that thy joy may be full.

D&C 59:13

See also Alma 5:46; 6:6; Hel. 3:35.

To discipline ourselves through fasting brings us in tune with God, and fast day provides an occasion to set aside the temporal so that we might enjoy the higher qualities of the spiritual. As we fast on that day we learn and better understand the needs of those who are less fortunate.

(Howard W. Hunter, "Fast Day," *Ensign*, Nov. 1985, 74.)

SEPTEMBER 21

Feeling the Peaceful Joy of the Book of Mormon

And I saw another angel fly in the midst of heaven, having the everlasting gospel to preach unto them that dwell on the earth, and to every nation, and kindred, and tongue, and people.

Rev. 14:6

See also D&C 17:6; 20:8–12; Moro. 10:3–5. *[Note that 21 September 1823 marked the first appearance of the Angel Moroni to Joseph Smith.]*

There is an inspiration and feeling of peaceful joy and satisfaction which accompany the sincere and prayerful reading of [the Book of Mormon]. Its doctrines and literary merit are in keeping with the writings of the Jewish prophets. The sincere student who is willing to put Moroni's promise to the test is forced to say, "Surely this is the work of the Lord and not the work of man, for no man could have written it."

(Joseph Fielding Smith, *Doctrines of Salvation*, 3 vols., ed. Bruce R. McConkie [Salt Lake City: Bookcraft, 1954–56], 3:209.)

SEPTEMBER 22
Ponder and Meditate

Meditate upon these things; give thyself wholly to them; that thy profiting may appear to all.

1 TIM. 4:15

See also Ps. 119:18; Prov. 4:26; 2 Ne. 4:15.

I recall so vividly President McKay in his old age in a meeting with his counselors and the Twelve saying, "Brethren, we need to take more time to meditate, to think quietly."

(Gordon B. Hinckley, *Teachings of Gordon B. Hinckley* [Salt Lake City: Deseret Book, 1997], 334.)

SEPTEMBER 23

Having Hope in the Resurrection

But this I confess unto thee, that after the way which they call heresy, so worship I the God of my fathers, believing all things which are written in the law and in the prophets:

And have hope toward God, which they themselves also allow, that there shall be a resurrection of the dead, both of the just and unjust.

ACTS 24:14–15

See also Luke 14:14; 2 Ne. 25:11–19.

The "lively hope" we are given by the resurrection is our conviction that death is not the conclusion of our identity but merely a necessary step in the destined transition from mortality to immortality. This hope changes the whole perspective of mortal life. The assurance of resurrection and immortality affects how we look on the physical challenges of mortality, how we live our mortal lives, and how we relate to those around us.

(Dallin H. Oaks, "Resurrection," *Ensign*, May 2000, 14.)

SEPTEMBER 24

Hungering and Thirsting after Righteousness

And blessed are all they who do hunger and thirst after righteousness, for they shall be filled with the Holy Ghost.

3 NE. 12:6

See also Acts 10:35; 1 Tim. 6:11; D&C 20:14.

As I have thought about the serious sins that some of our members have committed, I have wondered, Did they seek the Lord to help them overcome their emotional outbursts or lascivious desires? Did they rely on fasting and prayer? Did they seek a priesthood blessing? Did they ask our Heavenly Father to temper their emotions by the influence of the Holy Ghost? Jesus said we are to "hunger and thirst after righteousness" (3 Ne. 12:6). To do this, we must earnestly desire a righteous and virtuous life.

(Ezra Taft Benson, *Come unto Christ* [Salt Lake City: Deseret Book, 1983], 51.)

SEPTEMBER 25

Searching for Happiness

Behold, happy is the man whom God correcteth: therefore despise not thou the chastening of the Almighty.

JOB 5:17

See also Alma 44:5; 4 Ne. 1:16; Morm. 7:7.

Although "men are, that they might have joy" (2 Ne. 2:25), this does not mean that our lives will be filled only with joy, "for it must needs be, that there is an opposition in all things" (2 Ne. 2:11). Happiness is not given to us in a package that we can just open up and consume. Nobody is ever happy 24 hours a day, seven days a week. Rather than thinking in terms of a day, we perhaps need to snatch happiness in little pieces, learning to recognize the elements of happiness and then treasuring them while they last.

(James E. Faust, "Our Search for Happiness," *Ensign*, Oct. 2000, 2.)

SEPTEMBER 26

Temple Blessings

The more sure word of prophecy means a man's knowing that he is sealed up unto eternal life, by revelation and the spirit of prophecy, through the power of the Holy Priesthood.

D&C 131:5

See also D&C 59:9; 110:7–8; 138:47–54.

Temple ordinances, covenants, endowments, and sealings enable individuals to be reconciled with the Lord and families to be sealed beyond the veil of death. Obedience to temple covenants qualifies us for eternal life, the greatest gift of God to man (see D&C 14:7). Eternal life is more than immortality. Eternal life is exaltation in the highest heaven—the kind of life that God lives.

(Russell M. Nelson, "Personal Preparation for Temple Blessings," *Ensign*, May 2001, 32.)

SEPTEMBER 27

Freedom through Forgiveness

And it came to pass that I did frankly forgive them all that they had done, and I did exhort them that they would pray unto the Lord their God for forgiveness. And it came to pass that they did so. And after they had done praying unto the Lord we did again travel on our journey towards the tent of our father.

1 NE. 7:21

See also John 13:35; Moro 6:8; JS–H 1:29.

The spirit must be freed from tethers so strong and feelings never put to rest, so that the lift of life may give buoyancy to the soul.

(Thomas S. Monson, "Hidden Wedges," *Ensign*, May 2002, 19.)

I baptize thee, having authority from the Almighty God, as a testimony that ye have entered into a covenant to serve him until you are dead as to the mortal body; and may the Spirit of the Lord be poured out upon you; and may he grant unto you eternal life, through the redemption of Christ, whom he has prepared from the foundation of the world.

MOSIAH 18:13

See also 1 Ne. 15:18; D&C 88:131–133.

All Latter-day Saints enter the new and everlasting covenant when they enter this Church. They covenant to cease sustaining, upholding and cherishing the kingdom of the Devil and the kingdoms of this world. They enter the new and everlasting covenant to sustain the Kingdom of God and no other kingdom. They take a vow of the most solemn kind, before the heavens and earth, and that, too, upon the validity of their own salvation, that they will sustain truth and righteousness instead of wickedness and falsehood, and build up the Kingdom of God, instead of the kingdoms of this world.

(Brigham Young, *Discourses of Brigham Young*, sel. John A. Widtsoe [Salt Lake City: Deseret Book, 1954], 160.)

Commit thy way unto the Lord; trust also in him; and he shall bring it to pass.

Ps. 37:5

See also 1 Sam. 12:24; 2 Kings 23:3; 1 Ne. 3:7.

We as individuals and families need to counsel together to carefully examine ourselves and our personal and family commitment to the gospel of Jesus Christ. This examination is particularly essential to those of us who have made covenants of consecration and sacrifice in the house of the Lord. We need to ask ourselves: Are we setting an example of Christian virtue and gospel faithfulness in our lives and in our homes? Are we reaching out to *our* inactive and nonmember friends, family members, and neighbors with loving concern? Are we boldly sharing our testimonies?

(M. Russell Ballard, "Are We Keeping Pace?" *Ensign*, Nov. 1998, 6.)

SEPTEMBER 30
The Law and Blessings of the Fast

And on this day thou shalt do none other thing, only let thy food be prepared with singleness of heart that thy fasting may be perfect, or, in other words, that thy joy may be full.

D&C 59:13

See also Alma 5:46; 17:3; Hel. 3:35.

As members of the Church, we have a sacred responsibility to assist those in need and to help relieve their heavy burdens. Observance of the law of the fast can help all people of all nations.

(Joseph B. Wirthlin, "The Law of the Fast," *Ensign*, May 2001, 73.)

OCTOBER

Therefore give heed to my words . . .

—3 Nephi 23:4

OCTOBER 1

Becoming Perfect

Therefore I would that ye should be perfect even as
I, or your Father who is in heaven is perfect.

3 Ne. 12:48

See also Matt. 5:48; 19:21; Heb. 6:1; D&C 76:69.

This progress toward eternal life is a matter of
achieving perfection. Living all the commandments
guarantees total forgiveness of sins and assures one of
exaltation through that perfection which comes by
complying with the formula the Lord gave us. In his
Sermon on the Mount he made the command to all
men: "Be ye therefore perfect, even as your Father
which is in heaven is perfect" (Matt. 5:48). Being
perfect means to triumph over sin. This is a mandate
from the Lord. He is just and wise and kind. He
would never require anything from his children
which was not for their benefit and which was not
attainable. Perfection therefore is an achievable goal.

(Spencer W. Kimball, *The Miracle of Forgiveness*, [Salt Lake
city: Bookcraft, 1969, 208–209.)

OCTOBER 2
Hold Out Faithful to the End

And moreover, I would desire that ye should consider on the blessed and happy state of those that keep the commandments of God. For behold, they are blessed in all things, both temporal and spiritual; and if they hold out faithful to the end they are received into heaven, that thereby they may dwell with God in a state of never–ending happiness. O remember, remember that these things are true; for the Lord God hath spoken it.

MOSIAH 2:41

See also Rom. 2:7; D&C 93:1; Matt. 5:7.

Patience is heavenly, obedience is noble, forgiveness is merciful, and exaltation is godly; and he that holds out faithful to the end shall in no wise lose his reward.

(Joseph Smith, *History of The Church of Jesus Christ of Latter-day Saints*, 7 vols., ed. B. H. Roberts [Salt Lake City: The Church of Jesus Christ of Latter-day Saints, 1932-1951], 6:427.)

OCTOBER 3

So Jesus had compassion on them, and touched their eyes: and immediately their eyes received sight, and they followed him.

MATT 20:34

See also 1 Cor. 11:1; Eph. 2:10; Morm. 7:10.

When Jesus walked and taught among men, He spoke in language easily understood. Whether He was journeying along the dusty way from Perea to Jerusalem, addressing the multitudes on the shore of the Sea of Galilee, or pausing beside Jacob's well in Samaria, He taught in parables. Jesus spoke frequently of having hearts that could know and feel, ears that were capable of hearing, and eyes that could truly see.

(Thomas S. Monson, "For I Was Blind but Now I See," *Ensign*, May 1999, 54.)

OCTOBER 4
Guiding Zion

And I have put my words in thy mouth, and I have covered thee in the shadow of mine hand, that I may plant the heavens, and lay the foundations of the earth, and say unto Zion, Thou art my people.

ISA. 51:16

See also Ps. 69:35; 92:2; Isa. 12:6.

We talk of a Zion that is to be built up. If a Zion is ever built up on this earth, it will have to be under the guidance and direction of the Almighty. . . . There is no man living in and of himself, can guide the ship of Zion or regulate the affairs of the Church and kingdom of God unaided by the Spirit of God, and hence he has organized the Church as he has with all the various quorums and organizations as they exist today.

(John Taylor, *The Gospel Kingdom: Selections from the Writings and Discourses of John Taylor*, sel. with an introduction by G. Homer Durham [Salt Lake City: Improvement Era, 1941], 38.)

OCTOBER 5
Using the Lifeline of Prayer

Behold, verily, verily, I say unto you, ye must watch and pray always lest ye enter into temptation; for Satan desireth to have you, that he may sift you as wheat.

3 NE. 18:18

See also 1 Ne. 15:7–11; 3 Ne. 13:5–13.

Each of us has problems that we cannot solve and weaknesses that we cannot conquer without reaching out through prayer to a higher source of strength. That source is the God of heaven to whom we pray in the name of Jesus Christ. As we pray we should think of our Father in Heaven as possessing all knowledge, understanding, love, and compassion.

(James E. Faust, "The Lifeline of Prayer," *Ensign*, May 2002, 59.)

OCTOBER 6
Priesthood Power

Therefore, in the ordinances thereof, the power of godliness is manifest.

And without the ordinances thereof, and the authority of the priesthood, the power of godliness is not manifest unto men in the flesh.

D&C 84:20–21

See also D&C 107:17–18, 79; 112:30; 128:8.

Through its power, worlds—even universes—have, are, and will be created or organized. Through its power, ordinances are performed which, when accompanied by righteousness, allow families to be together forever, sins to be forgiven, the sick to be healed, the blind to see, and even life to be restored.

(John H. Groberg, "Priesthood Power," *Ensign*, May 2001, 43.)

Remember faith, virtue, knowledge, temperance, patience, brotherly kindness, godliness, charity, humility, diligence.

D&C 4:6

See also Moro. 7:5–17; Ether 4:11–12.

Good men, well-intentioned men of great capacity, trade character for trinkets that turn to wax before their eyes and dreams that become only haunting nightmares. How rare a gem, how precious a jewel is the man or woman in whom there is neither guile nor deception nor falsehood! . . . We cannot be less than honest, we cannot be less than true, we cannot be less than virtuous if we are to keep sacred the trust given us.

(Gordon B. Hinckley, "An Honest Man—God's Noblest Work," *Ensign*, May 1976, 62.)

OCTOBER 8
Teach and Live the Gospel

Even so hath the Lord ordained that they which preach the gospel should live of the gospel.

1 COR. 9:14

See also Rom. 1:15–16; 3 Ne. 27:21; 28:23; D&C 103:9.

I ask every man and woman occupying a place of responsibility whose duty it is to teach the gospel of Jesus Christ to live it and keep the commandments of God, so that their example will teach it. . . . No man can teach the gospel of Jesus Christ under the inspiration of the living God and with power from on high unless he is living it.

(Heber J. Grant, *Gospel Standards: Selections from the Sermons and Writings of Heber J. Grant*, comp. G. Homer Durham [Salt Lake City: Improvement Era, 1981], 72.)

OCTOBER 9
Parents' Example

For I have given you an example, that ye should do as I have done to you.

JOHN 13:15

See also 1 Tim. 4:7; Jacob 2:35; 3 Ne. 15:12.

If parents will continually set before their children examples worthy of their imitation and the approval of our Father in Heaven, they will turn the current, and the tide of feelings of their children, and they, eventually, will desire righteousness more than evil.

(Brigham Young, *Discourses of Brigham Young*, sel. John A. Widtsoe [Salt Lake City: Deseret Book, 1954], 208.)

OCTOBER 10
Humility Is a Virtue

And blessed are the meek, for they shall inherit the earth.

3 Ne. 12:5

See also Alma 37:33; Moro. 7:44; 8:26.

Humility is a virtue. One who possesses it is teachable and amenable to instruction. You should, therefore, be humble and "hunger and thirst after righteousness" so that your abilities may be developed, your gifts cultivated, your skills polished, and your confidence increased. In the process, you will "be filled with the Holy Ghost" and strengthened in your calling (3 Ne. 12:6).

(Carlos E. Asay, *In the Lord's Service: A Guide to Spiritual Development* [Salt Lake City: Deseret Book, 1990], 1.)

OCTOBER 11
Living by His Words of Power

But the Lord knoweth all things from the beginning; wherefore, he prepareth a way to accomplish all his works among the children of men; for behold, he hath all power unto the fulfilling of all his words. And thus it is. Amen.

1 NE. 9:6

See also Luke 4:32; Heb. 6:5; D&C 131:5.

Salvation is not in facilities or technology, but in the word. Only in the power of the word will it impact our lives and help us to live closer to our Father in Heaven.

(L. Tom Perry, "Thou Shalt Give Heed unto all His Words," *Ensign*, May 2000, 25.)

OCTOBER 12
Bearing a Fervent Testimony

For I know that my redeemer liveth, and that he shall stand at the latter day upon the earth.

JOB 19:25

See also John 7:17; 8:32; 17:3; 1 Cor. 1:6; 12:3.

When I heard the Gospel I knew it was true. When I first read the Book of Mormon, I knew it was inspired of God; when I first beheld Joseph Smith I knew I stood face to face with a prophet of the living God, and I had no doubt in my mind about his authority.

(Bathsheba B. Smith, quoted in Janet Peterson and LaRene Gaunt, *Elect Ladies* [Salt Lake City: Deseret Book, 1990], 76.)

OCTOBER 13
Assurance of Eternal Life

Search the scriptures; for in them ye think ye have eternal life: and they are they which testify of me.

JOHN 5:39

See also 1 Jn. 5:11, 13; D&C 6:7; 42:61; 68:12.

I wish that all of the people of the world—all our Father's children—could understand the scriptures that have been given to us by the Lord and preserved by the Lord and preserved by his servants. They are replete with assurance of the resurrection and of eternal life. Of course the outstanding evidence was that of Jesus Christ our Lord who was crucified at Calvary, removed from the cross, and laid away in a tomb. Those witnessing this great event supposed that would be the last time they would ever see him, but in three days he left the tomb, in three days his spirit had entered his immortal tabernacle, and he was among his associates again.

(George Albert Smith, *The Teachings of George Albert Smith*, ed. Robert McIntosh and Susan McIntosh [Salt Lake City: Bookcraft, 1996], 9.)

OCTOBER 14
We Covenant to Do Good

And it came to pass that I, Nephi, beheld the power of the Lamb of God, that it descended upon the saints of the church of the Lamb, and upon the covenant people of the Lord, who were scattered upon all the face of the earth; and they were armed with righteousness and with the power of God in great glory.

1 Ne. 14:14

See also 2 Ne. 9:1–2; D&C 82:14; 101:39–42.

We are a covenant people. We covenant to give of our resources in time and money and talent—all we are and all we possess—to the interest of the kingdom of God upon the earth. In simple terms, we covenant to do good. We are a covenant people, and the temple is the center of our covenants. It is the source of the covenant.

(Boyd K. Packer, *The Holy Temple* [Salt Lake City: Bookcraft, 1980], 170.)

OCTOBER 15

And behold, I tell you these things that ye may learn wisdom; that ye may learn that when ye are in the service of your fellow beings ye are only in the service of your God.

MOSIAH 2:17

See also Matt. 16:15; Mosiah 4:15; D&C 4:2.

The followers of the divine Christ have to be weighed on the scales of what their actions are rather than on solemn professions of belief. The true measure is found in Matthew: "Inasmuch as ye have done it unto one of the least of these . . . ye have done it unto me" (Matt. 25:40). A wise man observed, "The man who lives by himself and for himself is apt to be corrupted by the company he keeps" (Charles Henry Parkhurst).

(James E. Faust, *To Reach Even unto You* [Salt Lake City: Deseret Book, 1980], 109.)

OCTOBER 16

A Most Undeviating Friend

Henceforth I call you not servants; for the servant knoweth not what his lord doeth: but I have called you friends; for all things that I have heard of my Father I have made known unto you.

JOHN 15:15

See also Prov. 17:17; 18:24; D&C 88:133.

How far you are capable of being "a most undeviating friend, without being governed by the smallest religious influence," will best be decided by your survivors, as all past experience most assuredly proves. Without controversy, that friendship which intelligent beings would accept as sincere must arise from love, and that love grow out of virtue, which is as much a part of religion as light is a part of Jehovah. Hence the saying of Jesus, "Greater love hath no man than this, that a man lay down his life for his friends."

(Joseph Smith, *History of The Church of Jesus Christ of Latter-day Saints*, 7 vols., ed. B. H. Roberts [Salt Lake City: The Church of Jesus Christ of Latter-day Saints, 1932–1951], 6: 73.)

OCTOBER 17
Faithfully Doing the Will of God

For you shall live by every word that proceedeth forth from the mouth of God.

D&C 84:44

See also Mosiah 2:22; D&C 20:77; 43:8.

And now all the Latter-day Saints have to do, all that is required of us to make us perfectly safe under all circumstances of trouble or persecution, is to do the will of God: to be honest, faithful, and to keep ourselves devoted to the principles that we have received; do right one by another; trespass upon no man's rights; live by every word that proceedeth from the mouth of God, and His Holy Spirit will aid and assist us under all circumstances, and we will come out of the midst of it all abundantly blessed.

(Lorenzo Snow, *The Teachings of Lorenzo Snow*, ed. Clyde J. Williams [Salt Lake City: Bookcraft, 1984], 11.)

OCTOBER 18

Undershepherds of the Lord

O Lord, wilt thou grant unto us that we may have success in bringing them again unto thee in Christ.

Behold, O Lord, their souls are precious, and many of them are our brethren; therefore, give unto us, O Lord, power and wisdom that we may bring these, our brethren, again unto thee.

ALMA 31:34–35

See also John 21:15–17; D&C 81:5; 108:7.

The Lord, our Good Shepherd, expects us to be his undershepherds and recover those who are struggling or are lost. We can't tell you how to do it, but as you become involved and seek inspiration, success will result from efforts in your areas, stakes, and wards.

(Howard W. Hunter, *The Teachings of Howard W. Hunter*, ed. Clyde J. Williams [Salt Lake City: Bookcraft, 1997], 218.)

OCTOBER 19
Daily Repentance

Repent ye therefore, and be converted, that your sins may be blotted out, when the times of refreshing shall come from the presence of the Lord.

ACTS 3:19

See also Alma 5:31–33; 34:15–17.

We must repent daily. In order for good to blossom it must be cultivated and exercised by constant practice, and to be truly righteous there is required a daily pruning of the evil growth of our characters by a daily repentance from sin.

(Harold B. Lee, *The Teachings of Harold B. Lee*, ed. Clyde J. Williams [Salt Lake City: Bookcraft, 1996], 113.)

OCTOBER 20
The Power of Correct Principles

Be not deceived; God is not mocked: for whatsoever a man soweth, that shall he also reap.

GAL. 6:7

See also Amos 3:2; Luke 16:2; D&C 82:10.

All of the self-inflicted tragedy that occurs today
from violation of the Lord's commandments could be
avoided by careful, consistent observance of revealed
truth. The productive power of correct principles can
make your life a joyous, satisfying experience.

(Richard G. Scott, "The Power of Correct Principles,"
Ensign, May 1993, 32.)

OCTOBER 21
What Do You Seek?

Wherefore, seek not the things of this world but seek ye first to build up the kingdom of God, and to establish his righteousness, and all these things shall be added unto you.

JST, Matt. 6:38

See also 1 Ne. 8:30; D&C 30:18–21; 103:36.

Man's success or failure, happiness or misery, depends upon what he seeks and what he chooses. What a man is, what a nation is, may largely be determined by his or its dominant quest. It is a tragic thing to carry through life a low concept of it.

(David O. McKay, *Gospel Ideals: Selections from the Discourses of David O. McKay* [Salt Lake City: Improvement Era, 1953], 491.)

OCTOBER 22

Cultivating Divine Attributes

Whereby are given unto us exceeding great and precious promises: that by these ye might be partakers of the divine nature, having escaped the corruption that is in the world through lust.

2 PET. 1:4

See also 2 Pet. 1:5–12; Moro. 7:48; D&C 4:6.

When we keep the Lord's commandments, faith, hope, and charity abide with us. These virtues "distil upon [our] soul as the dews from heaven" (D&C 121:45), and we prepare ourselves to stand with confidence before our Lord and Savior, Jesus Christ, "without blemish and without spot" (1 Pet. 1:19).

(Joseph B. Wirthlin, "Cultivating Divine Attributes," *Ensign*, Nov. 1998, 25.)

OCTOBER 23
Goodly Fathers

I, Nephi, having been born of goodly parents, therefore I was taught somewhat in all the learning of my father; and having seen many afflictions in the course of my days, nevertheless, having been highly favored of the Lord in all my days; yea, having had a great knowledge of the goodness and the mysteries of God, therefore I make a record of my proceedings in my days.

1 NE. 1:1

See also 1 Ne. 5:4; 2 Ne. 2:3; 6:3.

What, then, is a father's specific responsibility within the sacred walls of his home? May I suggest two basic responsibilities of every father in Israel. First, you have a sacred responsibility to provide for the material needs of your family. Second, you have a sacred responsibility to provide spiritual leadership in your family.

(Ezra Taft Benson, *Come, Listen to a Prophet's Voice* [Salt Lake City: Deseret Book, 1990], 39–42.)

OCTOBER 24

Consecrating the Spirit of Gathering

And it shall come to pass, that whosoever shall call on the name of the Lord shall be delivered: for in mount Zion and in Jerusalem shall be deliverance, as the Lord hath said, and in the remnant whom the Lord shall call.

JOEL 2:32

See also 2 Ne. 29:11–14; Matt. 18:20; John 11:52.

Now, O Lord! Thy servant has been obedient to the heavenly vision which Thou gavest him in his native land; and under the shadow of Thine outstretched arm, he has safely arrived in this place to dedicate and consecrate this land unto Thee, for the gathering together of Judah's scattered remnants, according to the predictions of the holy Prophets—for the building up of Jerusalem again after it has been trodden down by the Gentiles so long, and for rearing a Temple in honor of Thy name. Everlasting thanks be ascribed unto Thee, O Father, Lord of heaven and earth.

(Orson Hyde, in his dedicatory prayer on the Mount of Olives in Jerusalem, Sunday, 24 October 1841, Joseph Smith, *History of the Church*, 7 vols., ed. B.H. Roberts [Salt Lake City: The Church of Jesus Christ of Latter-day Saints, 1932–1951], 4:456.)

OCTOBER 25

Overcoming Fear

There is no fear in love; but perfect love casteth out fear: because fear hath torment. He that feareth is not made perfect in love.

1 Jn. 4:18

See also D&C 3:5–8; 38:30; 67:10.

Who among us can say that he or she has not felt fear? I know of no one who has been entirely spared. . . . We suffer from the fear of ridicule, the fear of failure, the fear of loneliness, the fear of ignorance. Some fear the present, some the future. Some carry the burden of sin and would give almost anything to unshackle themselves from those burdens but fear to change their lives. Let us recognize that fear comes not of God, but rather that this gnawing, destructive element comes from the adversary of truth and righteousness. Fear is the antithesis of faith. It is corrosive in its effects, even deadly.

(Gordon B. Hinckley, *Teachings of Gordon B. Hinckley* [Salt Lake City: Deseret Book, 1997], 220–221.)

OCTOBER 26
Measuring Our Success

This book of the law shall not depart out of thy mouth; but thou shalt meditate therein day and night, that thou mayest observe to do according to all that is written therein: for then thou shalt make thy way prosperous, and then thou shalt have good success.

JOSH. 1:8

See also Alma 17:4.

Time is the raw material of life. Every day unwraps itself like a gift, bringing us the opportunity to spin a fabric of health, pleasure, and content and to evolve into something better than we are at its beginning. Success is contingent upon our effective use of the time given us. . . . Success is the ratio of our accomplishments to our capacities.

(Thomas S. Monson, *Pathways to Perfection* [Salt Lake City: Deseret Book, 1973], 110.)

OCTOBER 27
Being Enthusiastic

But it is good to be zealously affected always in a
good thing, and not only when I am present with you.

GAL. 4:18

See also Alma 21:23; 27:27.

Happiness, enthusiasm, and joy in daily living
are mandatory if we would move forward and choose
the good part. The principles of the gospel of Jesus
Christ will never change, but environment, circumstances, institutions, and cultural patterns do. Our
challenge is to move forward in our present realms
with commitment and enthusiasm.

(Marvin J. Ashton, *Be of Good Cheer* [Salt Lake City: Deseret
Book, 1987], 25.)

OCTOBER 28
Personal Temple Worship

And now, my dearly beloved brethren and sisters, let me assure you that these are principles in relation to the dead and the living that cannot be lightly passed over, as pertaining to our salvation. For their salvation is necessary and essential to our salvation, as Paul says concerning the fathers—that they without us cannot be made perfect—neither can we without our dead be made perfect.

D&C 128:15

See also D&C 2:2; 110:12; 128:18; Moses 6:8.

Regular temple attendance is one of the simplest ways you can bless those who are waiting in the spirit world. If you live near a temple, partake of the opportunity to go *often* and *regularly.* If you live some distance from a temple, plan excursions so that you, too, might be uplifted and edified through this most satisfying and much-needed labor of love.

(David B. Haight, "Personal Temple Worship," *Ensign,* May 1993, 23.)

Perspective on Humility

Be not ashamed, neither confounded; but be admonished in all your high-mindedness and pride, for it bringeth a snare upon your souls.

D&C 90:17

See also 1 Ne. 11:36; 2 Ne. 28:12; Jacob 2:16.

Another helpful perspective on humility can be obtained by examining its antithesis—pride. Just as humility leads to other virtues such as modesty, teachableness, and unpretentiousness, pride leads to many other vices. In Latter-day Saint theology, it was through pride that Satan became the adversary of all truth. It was the growth of this arrogance, termed *hubris,* that the wise men of ancient Greece portrayed as the sure road to destruction.

(Marlin K. Jensen, "To Walk Humbly with Thy God," *Ensign*, May 2001, 9.)

OCTOBER 30
Intent of Our Hearts

And it is requisite with the justice of God that men should be judged according to their works; and if their works were good in this life, and the desires of their hearts were good, that they should also, at the last day, be restored unto that which is good.

ALMA 41:3

See also Mosiah 18:10, 12; Moro. 7:9; 10:4.

In the great plan of salvation nothing has been overlooked. The gospel of Jesus Christ is the most beautiful thing in the world. It embraces every soul whose heart is right and who diligently seeks him and desires to obey his laws and covenants. Therefore, if a person is for any cause denied the privilege of complying with any of the covenants, the Lord will judge him or her by the intent of the heart.

(Dallin H. Oaks, *Pure in Heart* [Salt Lake City: Bookcraft, 1988], 62.)

OCTOBER 31

The Savior Will Succor His People

And he shall go forth, suffering pains and afflictions and temptations of every kind; and this that the word might be fulfilled which saith he will take upon him the pains and the sicknesses of his people.

ALMA 7:11

See also D&C 84:85–88; 88:6; 93:9.

When those difficult times come to us, we can remember that Jesus had to descend below all things before he could ascend above them, and that he suffered pains and afflictions and temptations of every kind that he might be filled with mercy and know how to succor his people in their infirmities.

(Jeffrey R. Holland, "This Do in Remembrance of Me," *Ensign*, Nov. 1995, 69.)

NOVEMBER

*Many . . . were baptized
in the name of Jesus.*

—3 Nephi 26:17

NOVEMBER 1

Put the Lord's Kingdom First

Blessed are ye for this thing which ye have done, for this is fulfilling my commandments, and this doth witness unto the Father that ye are willing to do that which I have commanded you.

3 NE. 18:10

See also JST, Matt.6:38,D&C 18:5; 31:5; 65:2.

We do not have to be called to serve far from home, nor do we have to hold a prominent place in the Church or in the world to build up the Lord's kingdom. We build it in our own hearts as we cultivate the Spirit of God in our lives. We build it within our families by instilling faith in our children. And we build it through the organization of the Church as we magnify our callings and share the gospel with neighbors and friends.

(Bruce D. Porter, "Building the Kingdom," *Ensign*, May 2001, 80.)

NOVEMBER 2
Maintaining a Positive Attitude

Wherefore, whoso believeth in God might with surety hope for a better world, yea, even a place at the right hand of God, which hope cometh of faith, maketh an anchor to the souls of men, which would make them sure and steadfast, always abounding in good works, being led to glorify God.

ETHER 12:4

See also Prov. 23:7; 1 Jn. 3:3; Moro. 7:6–8.

The Savior reminds us, "All things are possible to him that believeth" (Mark 9:23), and "All things shall work together for your good" (D&C 90:24). The attitude with which we submit to "all things" is important. Maintaining a positive attitude and being cheerful are helpful. A belief that "all these things shall give thee experience, and shall be for thy good" is like a spiritual stabilizer (D&C 122:7).

(James E. Faust, *Reach Up for the Light* [Salt Lake City: Deseret Book, 1990], 83.)

NOVEMBER 3
Love of God, Love for All

And hope maketh not ashamed; because the love of God is shed abroad in our hearts by the Holy Ghost which is given unto us.

ROM. 5:5

See also John 13:34–35; 1 Thes. 4:9; 1 Jn. 2:10.

Love is one of the chief characteristics of Deity, and ought to be manifested by those who aspire to be the sons of God. A man filled with the love of God, is not content with blessing his family alone, but ranges through the whole world, anxious to bless the whole human race.

(Joseph Smith, *History of The Church of Jesus Christ of Latter-day Saints*, 7 vols., ed. B. H. Roberts [Salt Lake City: The Church of Jesus Christ of Latter-day Saints, 1932–1951], 4:227.)

NOVEMBER 4

Prayer Is a Key to Wisdom, Virtue, and Humility

But thou, when thou prayest, enter into thy closet, and when thou hast shut thy door, pray to thy Father which is in secret; and thy Father which seeth in secret shall reward thee openly.

MATT. 6:6

See also John 15:7; Philip. 4:6; 1 Ne. 15:11.

We will regard our body as a temple of our very own (see 1 Cor. 3:16). We will not let it be desecrated or defaced in any way (1 Cor. 3:17). . . . Should not equal attention be paid to spiritual fitness? (see 1 Cor. 9:24–27; Heb. 12:9) Just as physical strength requires exercise, so spiritual strength requires effort. Among the most important of spiritual exercises is prayer. It engenders harmony with God and a desire to keep His commandments. Prayer is a key to wisdom, virtue, and humility.

(Russell M. Nelson, "We Are Children of God," *Ensign*, Nov. 1998, 87.)

NOVEMBER 5

Restore Your Self-Respect

Remember the worth of souls is great in the sight of God.

D&C 18:10

See also Isa. 13:12; Alma 24:14; D&C 109:43.

A great psychologist, MacDougall, once said: "The first thing to be done to help a man to moral regeneration is to restore if possible his self-respect." Also I recall the prayer of the old English weaver, "O God, help me to hold a high opinion of myself." That should be the prayer of every soul; not an abnormally developed self-esteem that becomes haughtiness, conceit, or arrogance, but a righteous self-respect that might be defined as "belief in one's own worth, worth to God, and worth to man."

(Harold B. Lee, *Stand Ye in Holy Places* [Salt Lake City: Deseret Book, 1974], 6–7.)

NOVEMBER 6

True Doctrine, Understood, Changes Attitudes and Behavior

If any man will do his will, he shall know of the doctrine, whether it be of God, or whether I speak of myself.

JOHN 7:17

See also Philip. 4:8; Moro. 10:4; D&C 84:45.

True doctrine, understood, changes attitudes and behavior. The study of the doctrines of the gospel will improve behavior quicker than a study of behavior will improve behavior. Preoccupation with unworthy behavior can lead to unworthy behavior. That is why we stress so forcefully the study of the doctrines of the gospel.

(Boyd K. Packer, "Little Children," *Ensign*, Nov. 1986, 16.)

NOVEMBER 7

The Danger of Idleness

And withal they learn to be idle, wandering about from house to house; and not only idle, but tattlers also and busybodies, speaking things which they ought not.

1 TIM. 5:13

See also 1 Ne. 12:23; Alma 38:2; D&C 60:13.

The idle generation! Hours each day and nothing to do. Saturdays and nothing to do. Three long months of school vacation and nothing to do. No one has found a truer adage than: "The idle brain is the devil's workshop."

(Spencer W. Kimball, *The Teachings of Spencer W. Kimball*, ed. Edward L. Kimball [Salt Lake City: Bookcraft, 1982], 361.)

NOVEMBER 8
You Must Be Such a True Friend

I say unto you, Though he will not rise and give him, because he is his friend, yet because of his importunity he will rise and give him as many as he needeth.

LUKE 11:8

See also John 15:13–15; 2 Ne. 1:30; Mosiah 28:2.

All of us will be tested. And all of us need true friends to love us, to listen to us, to show us the way, and to testify of truth to us so that we may retain the companionship of the Holy Ghost. You must be such a true friend. I can still remember, as if it were today, friends who touched my life for good long ago. They are gone, but the memory of their love, example, faith, and testimony still lifts me. And your friendship to even one new member may, in this life and in the next, cause hundreds or even thousands of their ancestors and their descendants to call you blessed.

(Henry B. Eyring, "True Friends," *Ensign*, May 2002, 26.)

NOVEMBER 9
Remembering to Encourage and Praise

His lord said unto him, Well done, thou good and faithful servant: thou hast been faithful over a few things, I will make thee ruler over many things: enter thou into the joy of thy lord.

MATT. 25:21

See also Acts 10:33; D&C 70:17.

We enjoy life when we have the ability to praise others for their good works. George Matthew Adams said: "He who praises another, enriches himself more than he does the one praised. To praise is an investment in happiness. The poorest human being has something to give that the richest cannot buy."

(Howard W. Hunter, BYU *Speeches of the Year*, Apr., 1961, 3.)

NOVEMBER 10
Doing Good Is of Great Value

Yea, a man may say, Thou hast faith, and I have works: shew me thy faith without thy works, and I will shew thee my faith by my works.

JAMES 2:18

See also Philip. 2:12; James 1:22; Mosiah 5:15.

We ought not to speak lightly of and undervalue the life we now enjoy. . . . the hours and minutes are spent in doing good. . . . in making ourselves useful, in improving our talents and abilities to do more good, cultivating the principle of kindness to every being pertaining to our earthly sphere. . . . learning to conduct ourselves towards our families and friends in a way to win the love and confidence of the good, and overcome every ungovernable passion by a constant practice of cool judgment and deliberate thoughts.

(Brigham Young, *Discourses of Brigham Young*, sel. John A. Widtsoe [Salt Lake City: Deseret Book, 1954], 91.)

NOVEMBER 11

Prayerfully Read the Book of Mormon

And now, as the preaching of the word had a great tendency to lead the people to do that which was just—yea, it had had more powerful effect upon the minds of the people than the sword, or anything else, which had happened unto them—therefore Alma thought it was expedient that they should try the virtue of the word of God.

ALMA 31:5

See also 1 Ne. 13:29; D&C 18:34–36.

Brothers and sisters, without reservation I promise you that if you will prayerfully read the Book of Mormon, regardless of how many times you previously have read it, there will come into your hearts an added measure of the Spirit of the Lord. There will come a strengthened resolution to walk in obedience to his commandments, and there will come a stronger testimony of the living reality of the Son of God.

(Gordon B. Hinckley, "The Power of the Book of Mormon," *Ensign*, June 1988, 6.)

NOVEMBER 12

Desiring Wisdom

And wisdom and knowledge shall be the stability of thy times, and strength of salvation: the fear of the Lord is his treasure.

Isa. 33:6

See also Mosiah 2:17; Alma 37:35; D&C 88:118.

First of all that I would crave as the richest of heaven's blessings would be wisdom from my Heavenly Father bestowed daily, so that whatever I might do or say, I could not look back at the close of the day with regret, nor neglect the performance of any act that would bring a blessing. . . . I particularly desire wisdom to bring up all the children that are, or may be committed to my charge, in such a manner that they will be useful ornaments in the Kingdom of God, and in a coming day arise up and call me blessed.

(Emma Hale Smith, quoted in Janet Peterson and LaRene Gaunt, *Elect Ladies* [Salt Lake City: Deseret Book, 1990], 17–18.)

NOVEMBER 13
Avoiding Unnecessary Stress

And I said, Oh that I had wings like a dove! for then would I fly away, and be at rest. Lo, then would I wander far off, and remain in the wilderness. Selah.

Ps. 55:6–7

See also Ps. 142:3–5; Alma 42:1.

The stress most faithful Church members feel arises out of the shared pressures of daily life, the temptations and afflictions common to mortals. These real pressures are unnecessarily increased when some unwisely place upon themselves unrealistic expectations. As to this avoidable stress, the Lord's instructions are very clear:

Do not run faster or labor more than you have strength and means provided to enable you to translate; but be diligent unto the end (D&C 10:4).

(Neal A. Maxwell, *Men and Women of Christ* [Salt Lake City: Bookcraft, 1991], 22.)

NOVEMBER 14

The Covenant of Baptism

Now this is the commandment: Repent, all ye ends of the earth, and come unto me and be baptized in my name, that ye may be sanctified by the reception of the Holy Ghost, that ye may stand spotless before me at the last day.

3 NE. 27:20

See also Heb. 6:2; D&C 112:29; Moses 6:59.

When we understand our baptismal covenant and the gift of the Holy Ghost, it will change our lives and will establish our total allegiance to the kingdom of God. When temptations come our way, if we will listen, the Holy Ghost will remind us that we have promised to remember our Savior and obey the commandments of God.

(Robert D. Hales, "The Covenant of Baptism: To Be in the Kingdom and of the Kingdom," *Ensign*, Nov. 2000, 6.)

NOVEMBER 15

Let Charity Crown Your Works

And be ye kind one to another, tenderhearted, forgiving one another, even as God for Christ's sake hath forgiven you.

EPH. 4:32

See also 1 Pet. 3:8; Moro. 7:45; D&C 121:42.

When you go home, never give a cross or unkind word to your husbands (or wives), but let kindness, charity and love crown your works henceforward; don't envy the finery and fleeting show of sinners, for they are in a miserable situation; but as far as you can, have mercy on them.

(Joseph Smith, *Teachings of the Prophet Joseph Smith*, sel. Joseph Fielding Smith [Salt Lake City: Deseret Book, 1976], 229.)

NOVEMBER 16

Celestial Glory

Wherefore, as it is written, they are gods, even the sons of God—Wherefore, all things are theirs, whether life or death, or things present, or things to come, all are theirs and they are Christ's, and Christ is God's. And they shall overcome all things.

D&C 76:58–60

See also 1 Cor. 15:40; 2 Cor. 12:2; D&C 88:22.

The Latter-day Saints have started out for celestial glory, and if we can only manage to be faithful enough to obtain an inheritance in the kingdom, where God and Christ dwell, we shall rejoice through the endless ages of eternity.

(Wilford Woodruff, *The Discourses of Wilford Woodruff*, ed. G. Homer Durham [Salt Lake City: Bookcraft, 1969], 262.)

NOVEMBER 17

The Brilliant Morning of Forgiveness

Behold, he who has repented of his sins, the same is forgiven, and I, the Lord, remember them no more.

By this ye may know if a man repenteth of his sins—behold, he will confess them and forsake them.

D&C 58:42–43

See also Enos 1:5; 3 Ne. 13:14: D&C 18:13.

The gospel teaches us that relief from torment and guilt can be earned through repentance. Save for those few who defect to perdition after having known a fulness, there is no habit, no addiction, no rebellion, no transgression, no offense exempted from the promise of complete forgiveness.

(Boyd K. Packer, "The Brilliant Morning of Forgiveness," *Ensign*, Nov. 1995, 18.)

NOVEMBER 18

Listening to the Voice of Living Prophets

For his word ye shall receive, as if from mine own mouth, in all patience and faith.

D&C 21:5

See also Amos 3:7; 3 Ne. 28:34–35; D&C 1:38.

"Is there one clear, unpolluted, unbiased voice that we can always count on? Is there a voice that will always give us clear directions to find our way in today's troubled world?" The answer is *yes*. That voice is the voice of the living prophet and apostles.

(M. Russell Ballard, "His Word Ye Shall Receive," *Ensign*, May 2001, 65.)

NOVEMBER 19
Seeking Cleanliness

Having therefore these promises, dearly beloved, let us cleanse ourselves from all filthiness of the flesh and spirit, perfecting holiness in the fear of God.

2 COR. 7:1

See also James 1:27; D&C 3:4.

The plaguing sin of this generation is sexual immorality. This, the Prophet Joseph said, would be the source of more temptations, more buffetings, and more difficulties for the elders of Israel than any other (See Journal of Discourses, 8:55).

(Ezra Taft Benson, *The Teachings of Ezra Taft Benson* [Salt Lake City: Bookcraft, 1988], 277.)

NOVEMBER 20
Establishing Purity and Virtue

Seeing ye have purified your souls in obeying the truth through the Spirit unto unfeigned love of the brethren, see that ye love one another with a pure heart fervently.

1 PET. 1:22

See also Matt. 5:8; Hel. 3:35; Moro. 7:48.

That is the mission of every man, from the President of the Church down to the latest convert in the Church. Every officer holds his position to build up, to bless; and, as President Joseph F. Smith has said, to establish righteousness, purity, and virtue among mankind.

(David O. McKay, *Gospel Ideals: Selections from the Discourses of David O. McKay* [Salt Lake City: Improvement Era, 1953], 143.)

NOVEMBER 21
A Powerful Testimony

Nevertheless, ye are blessed, for the testimony which ye have borne is recorded in heaven for the angels to look upon; and they rejoice over you, and your sins are forgiven you.

D&C 62:3

See also Alma 5:45–47; 30:41; Hel. 9:39.

Your testimony will be fortified as you exercise faith in Jesus Christ, in His teachings, and in His limitless power to accomplish what He has promised. . . . A powerful testimony distills from quiet moments of prayer and pondering as you recognize the impressions that will accompany such effort. Humble, trusting prayer brings consolation, solace, comfort, direction, and peace the unworthy can never know.

(Richard G. Scott, "The Power of a Strong Testimony," *Ensign*, Nov. 2001, 87–89.)

NOVEMBER 22
Teach and Train Our Children

And again, inasmuch as parents have children in Zion, or in any of her stakes which are organized, that teach them not to understand the doctrine of repentance, faith in Christ the Son of the living God, and of baptism and the gift of the Holy Ghost by the laying on of the hands, when eight years old, the sin be upon the heads of the parents.

D&C 68:25

See also Prov. 22:6; Mosiah 4:15; Alma 39:12.

If we do not take the pains to train our children, to teach and instruct them concerning these revealed truths, the condemnation will be upon us, as parents, or at least in a measure.

(Brigham Young, *Discourses of Brigham Young*, sel. John A. Widtsoe [Salt Lake City: Deseret Book, 1954], 207.)

NOVEMBER 23
Ye Are the Salt of the Earth

Verily, verily, I say unto you, I give unto you to be the salt of the earth; but if the salt shall lose its savor wherewith shall the earth be salted? The salt shall be thenceforth good for nothing, but to be cast out and to be trodden under foot of men.

3 Ne. 12:13

See also Mark 9:49–50; Luke 14:34.

The Savior's disciples are the salt of society in every dispensation. Salt preserves food from corruption and seasons it, making it wholesome and acceptable; in like manner the Master's disciples are to purify the society in which they move, setting a good example and counteracting every corrupt tendency.

(Harold B. Lee, *The Teachings of Harold B. Lee*, ed. Clyde J. Williams [Salt Lake City: Bookcraft, 1996], 615.)

NOVEMBER 24
Overcoming Difficult Situations

To him that overcometh will I grant to sit with me in my throne, even as I also overcame, and am set down with my Father in his throne.

REV. 3:21

See also D&C 61:9; 64:2; 76:53, 60.

The Lord has been good to me! Many, many times he has put ideas into my mind and even words into my mouth that have enabled me to meet difficult situations or remove resistant obstacles that otherwise might have impaired the work of the Society for which I had been given responsibility.

(Belle S. Spafford, quoted in Janet Peterson and LaRene Gaunt, *Elect Ladies* [Salt Lake City: Deseret Book, 1990], 160–161.)

NOVEMBER 25
The Design of Our Being

For behold, this is my work and my glory—to
bring to pass the immortality and eternal life of man.

MOSES 1:39

See also Gen. 1:26; 1 Jn. 3:1–2; D&C 76:24.

We are not here by chance. The Lord designed
our coming, and the object of our being. He designs
that we shall accomplish our mission, to become
conformed to the likeness and image of Jesus Christ,
that, like him, we may be without sin unto salvation,
like him we may be filled with pure intelligence, and
like him we may be exalted to the right hand of the
Father, to sit upon thrones and have dominion, and
power in the sphere in which we shall be called to act.
I testify to this doctrine, for the Lord has made me to
know and feel the truth of it from the crown of my
head to the soles of my feet.

(Joseph F. Smith, *Gospel Doctrine: Selections from the Sermons
and Writings of Joseph F. Smith*, comp. John A. Widtsoe [Salt Lake
City: Deseret Book, 1939], 5.)

NOVEMBER 26

Sisters Are Empowered to Glorify God

Let the saints be joyful in glory.

Ps. 149:5

See also D&C 138:39; Alma 56:47, 57:21.

Sisters received special gifts. They, according to the Lord, were empowered "to multiply and replenish the earth, according to my commandment, and to fulfil the promise which was given by my Father before the foundation of the world . . . for their exaltation in the eternal worlds, that they may bear the souls of men . . . herein is the work of my Father continued, that he may be glorified" (D&C 132:63). Think of it: When a mother bears and cares for a child, she not only helps the earth answer the end of its creation (see D&C 49:16–17), but she glorifies God!

(Russell M. Nelson, "How Firm Our Foundation," *Ensign*, May 2002, 75–76.)

NOVEMBER 27
Choosing to Feel the Blessings

And take upon you the name of Christ; that ye humble yourselves even to the dust, and worship God, in whatsoever place ye may be in, in spirit and in truth; and that ye live in thanksgiving daily, for the many mercies and blessings which he doth bestow upon you.

ALMA 34:38

See also Ps. 50:14; 2 Cor. 3:15; D&C 46:7.

Emptying out my desk, taking that last look around my office, I thought of all the events that had taken place in the beautiful Relief Society Building, events again so fresh in my mind as part of a soul-searing, soul-soaring experience. . . . So many people feel hurt when they are released from a position. I came to the conclusion when I was released that I could either be hurt or I could feel the blessings of those years. I chose to feel the blessings.

(Barbara Smith, as quoted in Janet Peterson and LaRene Gaunt, *Elect Ladies* [Salt Lake City: Deseret Book, 1990], 180.)

NOVEMBER 28
Using the Shield of Faith

Above all, taking the shield of faith, wherewith ye shall be able to quench all the fiery darts of the wicked.

EPH. 6:16

See also Alma 14:26; Ether 12:21; D&C 27:17.

Faith will be our strong shield to protect us from the fiery arrows of Satan. Values should not change with time, because faith in Jesus Christ is indispensable to happiness and eternal salvation.

(James E. Faust, "The Shield of Faith," *Ensign*, May 2000, 17.)

NOVEMBER 29

Heed the Voice of Warning

And the voice of warning shall be unto all people, by the mouths of my disciples, whom I have chosen in these last days.

D&C 1:4

See also 1 Ne. 4:6; 2 Ne. 32:5; D&C 100:5–6.

I promise you, if you will heed the voice of warning of the Holy Ghost and will follow His direction, you will be blessed with the ministering of angels, which will add wisdom, knowledge, power, and glory to your life. Remember, the Lord is bound by solemn covenant to bless our lives according to our faithfulness.

(L. Tom Perry, "Becoming Men in Whom the Spirit of God Is," *Ensign*, May 2002, 39.)

NOVEMBER 30

And blessed are all they who are persecuted for my name's sake, for theirs is the kingdom of heaven.

3 NE. 12:10

See also Matt. 5:12; Rom. 12:14; D&C 101:35.

Draw comfort from the words of the Master when we as a church are spoken of by those whose lives are torn with hate. They lash out at one thing and another. They manufacture and spread vile falsehoods behind which there is not a shred of truth. There is nothing new about this. But we shall go forward, returning good for evil, being helpful and kind and generous.

(Gordon B. Hinckley, *Stand A Little Taller*, [Salt Lake City: Eagle Gate, 2001], 23.)

DECEMBER

Believest thou that there is a God?

—ALMA 18:24

DECEMBER 1
Jesus Christ, the Son of God

The woman saith unto him, I know that Messias cometh, which is called Christ: when he is come, he will tell us all things.

JOHN 4:25

See also John 1:1–5; Acts 10:38; Mosiah 3:7–9.

Born in a stable, cradled in a manger, He came forth from heaven to live on earth as mortal man and to establish the kingdom of God. During His earthly ministry, He taught men the higher law. His glorious gospel reshaped the thinking of the world. He blessed the sick. He caused the lame to walk, the blind to see, the deaf to hear. He even raised the dead to life. One sentence from the book of Acts speaks volumes: Jesus 'went about doing good . . . for God was with him' (Acts 10:38).

(Thomas S. Monson, "They Showed the Way," *Ensign*, May 1997, 52.)

DECEMBER 2

To Look with Jealous Eyes

For jealousy is the rage of a man: therefore he will not spare in the day of vengeance.

PROV. 6:34

See also D&C 67:10.

He (Joseph) spoke of the disposition of many men to consider the lower offices in the Church dishonorable, and to look with jealous eyes upon the standing of others who are called to preside over them; that it was the folly and nonsense of the human heart for a person to be aspiring to other stations than those to which they are appointed of God for them to occupy; that it was better for individuals to magnify their respective calling.

(Joseph Smith, *Teachings of the Prophet Joseph Smith*, sel. Joseph Fielding Smith [Salt Lake City: Deseret Book, 1976], 223.)

DECEMBER 3

Christ Is Our Only Chance

Let your conversation be without covetousness; and be content with such things as ye have: for he hath said, I will never leave thee, nor forsake thee.

HEB. 13:5

See also Eph. 6:10; 1 Ne. 17:3.

The Lord has promised to heal our broken hearts and . . . to give power to the faint, to heal the wounded soul, and to turn our weakness into strength (see Isa. 40:29; Jacob 2:8; Ether 12:27); to take upon Him our pains and sicknesses, to blot out our transgressions if we repent, and loose the bands of death (see Alma 7:11–13). He promised that if we will build our lives upon His rock, the devil will have no power over us (see Hel. 5:12). And He has vowed that He will never leave us or forsake us (see Heb. 13:5). . . . He is our only chance.

(Sheri L. Dew, "Our Only Chance," *Ensign,* May 1999, 66.)

DECEMBER 4

Composition of Great Music

O sing unto the Lord a new song: sing unto the Lord, all the earth.

Sing unto the Lord, bless his name; shew forth his salvation from day to day.

Ps. 96:1–2

See also Ps. 100:1–2; Alma 5:26; D&C 128:122.

Someone [has] said, "Music is the language of the soul." I remembered what the Lord said in a revelation to Emma Smith, the wife of the Prophet, "For my soul delighteth in the song of the heart; yea, the song of the righteous is a prayer unto me, and it shall be answered with a blessing upon their heads" (D&C 25:12). There is truly no finer companion to true religion than great music.

(Harold B. Lee, *The Teachings of Harold B. Lee*, ed. Clyde J. Williams [Salt Lake City: Bookcraft, 1996], 203.)

DECEMBER 5

Rising above Afflictions

Many are the afflictions of the righteous: but the Lord delivereth him out of them all.

Ps. 34:19

See also 2 Cor 4:17; 1 Ne 18:16; 21:13; D&C 24:8.

It is necessary, then, that we pass through the school of suffering, trial, affliction, and privation, to know ourselves, to know others, and to know our God.

(John Taylor, *The Gospel Kingdom: Selections from the Writings and Discourses of John Taylor*, ed. G. Homer Durham [Salt Lake City: Improvement Era, 1941], 120.)

DECEMBER 6
Effective Leadership

But he that is greatest among you shall be your servant.

MATT. 23:11

See also Jarom 1:7; D&C 107:99–100.

A love of people is essential to effective leadership. Do you love those whom you work with? Do you realize the worth of souls is great in the sight of God (see D&C 18:10)? Do you have faith in youth? Do you find yourself praising their virtues, commending them for their accomplishments? Or do you have a critical attitude toward them because of their mistakes? One of the marks of great leadership always has been and ever will be the humble spirit.

(Ezra Taft Benson, *The Teachings of Ezra Taft Benson* [Salt Lake City: Bookcraft, 1988], 370.)

DECEMBER 7

Developing More Faith

But if ye will nourish the word, yea, nourish the tree as it beginneth to grow, by your faith with great diligence, and with patience, looking forward to the fruit thereof, it shall take root; and behold it shall be a tree springing up unto everlasting life.

ALMA 32:41

See also Heb. 11:1; 1 Pet. 1:7; Ether 12:6.

President Hinckley often speaks to us about developing more faith with our people. That faith is a result of our living the principles of the gospel, living the way we should and raising our children as we should, and seeing them grow and develop their character and personality in a way that they become an example of what we believe in and what we have a hope to do and accomplish.

(David B. Haight, "Faith of Our Prophets," *Ensign*, Nov. 2001, 24.)

DECEMBER 8
Treat All Mildly

Let all bitterness, and wrath, and anger, and clamour, and evil speaking, be put away from you, with all malice.

EPH. 4:31

See also Prov. 14:17; 15:18; Col. 3:21.

Our sufferings are permitted that we may learn by experience the contrast between good and evil, in order to obtain power; never suffer anger to find a seat in your breast, never get angry, treat all mildly, govern yourselves, control your passions, and it will give you power.

(Brigham Young, *Manuscript History of Brigham Young* [Salt Lake City: Church Archives], Millennial Star, vol. 26, 312.)

DECEMBER 9

Out of Darkness into His Marvelous Light

And that, knowing the time, that now it is high time to awake out of sleep: for now *is* our salvation nearer than when we believed.

The night is far spent, the day is at hand: let us therefore cast off the works of darkness, and let us put on the armour of light.

Rom. 13:11–12

See also Matt. 5:15–16; John 12:46; 2 Ne. 31:13.

Beloved young men and young women of the Church, we are engaged in a battle between the forces of light and darkness. If it were not for the Light of Jesus Christ and His gospel, we would be doomed to the destruction of darkness. But the Savior said, "I am come a light into the world" (John 12:46). "He that followeth me shall not walk in darkness, but shall have the light of life" (John 8:12).

(Robert D. Hales, "Out of Darkness into His Marvelous Light," *Ensign*, May 2002, 70.)

DECEMBER 10
Strengthening Our Faith

And the second is like unto it, Thou shalt love thy neighbour as thyself.

MATT. 22:39

See also Gal. 5:6; James 2:18; Enos 1:11.

Strengthening our faith by adding every good quality that adorns the children of the blessed Jesus, we can pray in the season of prayer; we can love our neighbor as ourselves, and be faithful in tribulation, knowing that the reward of such is greater in the kingdom of heaven. What a consolation! What a joy! Let me live the life of the righteous, and let my reward be like this!

(Joseph Smith, *History of The Church of Jesus Christ of Latter-day Saints*, 7 vols., ed. B. H. Roberts [Salt Lake City: The Church of Jesus Christ of Latter-day Saints, 1932–1951], 2:229.)

DECEMBER 11

Humility Is an Attribute of Godliness

Be thou humble; and the Lord thy God shall lead thee by the hand, and give thee answer to thy prayers.

D&C 112:10

See also Philip. 2:8; James 4:10; D&C 4:6.

Humility is an attribute of godliness possessed by true Saints. It is easy to understand why a proud man fails. He is content to rely upon himself only. This is evident in those who seek social position or who push others aside to gain position in fields of business, government, education, sports, or other endeavors. Our genuine concern should be for the success of others. The proud man shuts himself off from God, and when he does he no longer lives in the light.

(Howard W. Hunter, "The Pharisee and the Publican," *Ensign*, May 1984, 66.)

DECEMBER 12

Resolving to Improve Our Lives

Wherefore, whoso believeth in God might with surety hope for a better world, yea, even a place at the right hand of God, which hope cometh of faith, maketh an anchor to the souls of men, which would make them sure and steadfast, always abounding in good works, being led to glorify God.

ETHER 12:4

See also Moro. 6:3; Alma 1:25; 3 Ne. 6:14.

We are making, or should be making, an introspection into our present lives for the purpose of determining a course for the future. This looking into self will give us a clear outlook upon life from a true perspective. The outlook upon life is regulated by the "inlook" into self. From a complete self-analysis will come the New Year resolutions for future conduct.

(Matthew Cowley, *Matthew Cowley Speaks* [Salt Lake City: Deseret Book, 1954], 188.)

DECEMBER 13
Using Our Time Wisely

To every thing there is a season, and a time to every purpose under the heaven.

ECCL. 3:1

See also Eccl. 3:2–11; Alma 12:24; 42:4.

Our priorities are most visible in how we use our time. Someone has said, "Three things never come back—the spent arrow, the spoken word, and the lost opportunity." We cannot recycle or save the time allotted to us each day. With time, we have only one opportunity for choice, and then it is gone forever.

(Dallin H. Oaks, "Focus and Priorities," *Ensign*, May 2001, 83–84.)

DECEMBER 14

Moving Towards Exaltation

I will ascend above the heights of the clouds; I will be like the Most High.

2 NE 24:14

See also Ps. 3:3; John 21:24; Eph. 3:18.

We will change the world. For the better. For this journey to great heights is not any ordinary journey, any more than was Sariah's. Ours is a quest to change ourselves, to become even truer disciples of our Lord and Savior. We will lift our eyes to the mountains and move ceaselessly towards exaltation.

(Elaine L. Jack, "Look Up and Press On," *Ensign*, May 1992, 98.)

DECEMBER 15
Merciful Patience

In your patience possess ye your souls.

LUKE 21:19

See also Mosiah 3:19; D&C 24:8; 101:38.

Let us be more compassionate, gentler, filled with forbearance and patience and a greater measure of respect one for another. In so doing, our very example will cause others to be more merciful, and we shall have greater claim upon the mercy of God who in His love will be generous toward us.

(Gordon B. Hinckley, *Teachings of Gordon B. Hinckley* [Salt Lake City: Deseret Book, 1997], 338.)

DECEMBER 16
Know the Joy of Always Being a Missionary

And thou shalt teach them ordinances and laws, and shalt shew them the way wherein they must walk, and the work that they must do.

Ex. 18:20

See also Ps. 51:13; Matt. 28:19.

Do you remember the joy that comes from teaching the gospel to someone who has been deprived of these teachings throughout their life, the excitement that comes when you teach the law of the Lord, and the blessings that are received from following Him?

(L. Tom Perry, "The Returned Missionary," *Ensign*, Nov. 2001, 76.)

DECEMBER 17

Being Heirs of God

What is man, that thou art mindful of him? and the son of man, that thou visitest him?

For thou hast made him a little lower than the angels, and hast crowned him with glory and honour.

Ps. 8:4–5

See also Rom. 8:16–17; Alma 24:14; D&C 18:10.

We must remember, in a world where some still go hungry, that men, women, and children can starve from a lack of self-knowledge as much as they can from a lack of bread. That is why, when Jesus invited his disciples to partake of the emblems of his body and blood (3 Ne. 18:3–5), they were "filled"—filled with the spirit of heaven, filled with the spirit of hope, filled with more certain knowledge of who they really were—"heirs of God, and joint-heirs with Christ." That same spirit bears witness to us yet that we are the "children of God" (Rom. 8:17, 16).

(Jeffrey R. Holland, "Belonging: A View of Membership," *Ensign*, Apr. 1980, 31.)

DECEMBER 18
Selfless Service

And the King shall answer and say unto them, Verily I say unto you, Inasmuch as ye have done it unto one of the least of these my brethren, ye have done it unto me.

MATT. 25:40

See also Matt. 20:27; D&C 42:29; 81:5.

Rewards for selfless service were revealed by the Lord, who said, "Whosoever will save his life shall lose it: and whosoever will lose his life for my sake shall find it" (see Matt. 16:25).

(Russell M. Nelson, *Perfection Pending, and Other Favorite Discourses* [Salt Lake City: Deseret Book, 1998], 214.)

DECEMBER 19
Sacrifice of All Earthly Things

And ye shall offer for a sacrifice unto me a broken heart and a contrite spirit. And whoso cometh unto me with a broken heart and a contrite spirit, him will I baptize with fire and with the Holy Ghost, even as the Lamanites, because of their faith in me at the time of their conversion, were baptized with fire and with the Holy Ghost, and they knew it not.

3 NE. 9:20

See also 1 Sam. 15:22; 2 Ne. 2:7.

Let us here observe, that a religion that does not require the sacrifice of all things never has power sufficient to produce the faith necessary unto life and salvation . . . it was through this sacrifice, and this only, that God has ordained that men should enjoy eternal life; and it is through the medium of the sacrifice of all earthly things that men do actually know that they are doing the things that are well pleasing in the sight of God.

(Joseph Smith, *Lectures on Faith* [Salt Lake City: Deseret Book, 1985], 6:7.)

DECEMBER 20
Personal Improvement

Verily I say, men should be anxiously engaged in a good cause, and do many things of their own free will, and bring to pass much righteousness;

For the power is in them, wherein they are agents unto themselves. And inasmuch as men do good they shall in nowise lose their reward.

D&C 58:27–28

See also 3 Ne. 27:27; D&C 75:29.

Accept the reality that personal improvement on the part of each priesthood holder is expected by our Father in Heaven. We should be growing and we should be developing constantly. If we do, others will sense the seriousness of our discipleship and can then more easily forgive us our frailties which we sometimes show in the way in which we lead and manage.

(Spencer W. Kimball, *The Teachings of Spencer W. Kimball*, ed. Edward L. Kimball [Salt Lake City: Bookcraft, 1982], 175)

DECEMBER 21
Conversion and Happiness

If ye love me, keep my commandments.
JOHN 14:15

See also Mosiah 2:41; 5:2; 4 Ne. 1:15–16.

To be converted, you must remember to apply diligently in your life the key words "a love of God, with a fixed and controlling determination to keep his commandments" (Marion G. Romney, "According to the Covenants," in Conference Report, Guatemala Area Conference 1977, 8–9). Your happiness now and forever is conditioned on your degree of conversion and the transformation that it brings to your life.

(Richard G. Scott, "Full Conversion Brings Happiness," *Ensign*, May 2002, 25.)

DECEMBER 22

Nourishing Starving Spirits

And because of your diligence and your faith and your patience with the word in nourishing it, that it may take root in you, behold, by and by ye shall pluck the fruit thereof, which is most precious, which is sweet above all that is sweet, and which is white above all that is white, yea, and pure above all that is pure; and ye shall feast upon this fruit even until ye are filled, that ye hunger not, neither shall ye thirst.

ALMA 32:42

See also Ps. 85:11; Isa. 29:8; D&C 20:9; 42:12.

Amos prophesied of a "famine in the land, not a famine of bread, nor a thirst for water, but of hearing the words of the Lord" (Amos 8:11). The Book of Mormon: Another Testament of Jesus Christ has the nourishing power to heal starving spirits of the world.

(Boyd K. Packer, "The Book of Mormon: Another Testament of Jesus Christ," *Ensign*, Nov. 2001, 64.)

DECEMBER 23

A Chosen Seer

Yea, Joseph truly said: Thus saith the Lord unto me: A choice seer will I raise up out of the fruit of thy loins; and he shall be esteemed highly among the fruit of thy loins. And unto him will I give commandment that he shall do a work for the fruit of thy loins, his brethren, which shall be of great worth unto them, even to the bringing of them to the knowledge of the covenants which I have made with thy fathers.

2 NE. 3:7

See also D&C 1:17–22; 135:3.

The Lord raised up Joseph Smith specially to do the work that he performed. He was ordained and appointed before he was born to come upon the stage of action in this age of God's mercy to man, through the loins of ancient Joseph, who was a descendant of Abraham, Isaac, and Jacob, to lay the foundation of this great and glorious dispensation—a dispensation that will be marked and distinguished in the annals of human history for its grand and mighty, and also its serious and awful events.

(Wilford Woodruff, *The Discourses of Wilford Woodruff*, ed. G. Homer Durham [Salt Lake City: Bookcraft, 1969])

DECEMBER 24

Unconditional Love of God

For God so loved the world, that he gave his only begotten Son, that whosoever believeth in him should not perish, but have everlasting life.

JOHN 3:16

See also Alma 26:35; 4 Ne. 1:15–16; Ether 3:4.

Just as the love of God for us is unconditional, one day ours for Him will be likewise. This is what the first commandment is all about. But even then, the adoration and awe we have developed for God will take humble and eternal notice of the vital fact stressed by John—that God loved us first (1 John 4:19). Indeed, while God's great plan of redemption was made feasible by His omniscience and His omnipotence, it was made inevitable because of His perfect love for us!

(Neal A. Maxwell, *All These Things Shall Give Thee Experience* [Salt Lake City: Deseret Book, 1979], 128.)

DECEMBER 25
The Gift of Gratitude

Offer unto God thanksgiving; and pay thy vows unto the most High.

Ps. 50:14

See also Alma 34:38; D&C 46:7; 59:15.

Let us in our lives give to our Lord and Savior the gift of gratitude by living His teachings and following in His footsteps. It was said of Him that he "went about doing good." As we do likewise, the Christmas spirit will be ours.

(Thomas S. Monson, "Christmas Is Children, Remembering, Giving," *Church News, 14 Dec. 1996,*)

DECEMBER 26

Solace Abides through Prayer

If any of you lack wisdom, let him ask of God, that giveth to all men liberally, and upbraideth not; and it shall be given him.

But let him ask in faith, nothing wavering. For he that wavereth is like a wave of the sea driven with the wind and tossed.

JAMES 1:5–6

See also Alma 13:28; 17:3; Hel. 3:35.

Prayer will bring solace and comfort. It has healed sickness, comforted those distressed, and has continued the faithful in paths of righteousness. . . . Our great example in prayer is our Lord and Master Jesus Christ who knew that only through constant supplication and obedience would God the Father manifest His will and release the power for its attainment through man. Truly there is power in prayer.

(Ezra Taft Benson, *The Teachings of Ezra Taft Benson* [Salt Lake City: Bookcraft, 1988], 422.)

DECEMBER 27
Rewards of Integrity

Finally, brethren, whatsoever things are true, whatsoever things are honest, whatsoever things are just, whatsoever things are pure, whatsoever things are lovely, whatsoever things are of good report; if there be any virtue, and if there be any praise, think on these things.

PHILIP. 4:8

See also 2 Cor. 13:7; Heb. 13:18; D&C 11:10.

The rewards of integrity are immeasurable. One is the indescribable inner peace that comes from knowing we are doing what is right; another is an absence of the guilt and anxiety that accompany sin. . . . When we are doing what is right, we will not feel timid and hesitant about seeking divine direction. We will know that the Lord will answer our prayers and help us in our need. The consummate reward of integrity is the constant companionship of the Holy Ghost (see D&C 121:46).

(Joseph B. Wirthlin, *Finding Peace in Our Lives* [Salt Lake City: Deseret Book, 1995], 194.)

DECEMBER 28

God Is the Ultimate Source of Power

Yea, I know that I am nothing; as to my strength I am weak; therefore I will not boast of myself, but I will boast of my God, for in his strength I can do all things; yea, behold, many mighty miracles we have wrought in this land, for which we will praise his name forever.

ALMA 26:12

See also 3 Ne. 8:1; 4 Ne. 1:5; Ether 12:16.

The Lord can do remarkable miracles with a person of ordinary ability who is humble, faithful, and diligent in serving the Lord and seeks to improve himself. This is because God is the ultimate source of power.

(James E. Faust, "Acting for Ourselves and Not Being Acted Upon," *Ensign*, Nov. 1995, 45.)

DECEMBER 29
Filling Our Hearts with Love

See that ye love one another; cease to be covetous;
learn to impart one to another as the gospel requires.

D&C 88:123

See also Matt. 5:41; Mosiah 18:8–9; D&C 108:7.

My brothers and sisters, may we resolve from this
day forward to fill our hearts with love. May we go the
extra mile to include in our lives any who are lonely or
downhearted or who are suffering in any way. May we
"[cheer] up the sad and [make] someone feel glad"
("Have I done Any Good," *Hymns*, no. 223). May we
live so that when that final summons is heard, we may
have no serious regrets, no unfinished business, but
will be able to say with the Apostle Paul, "I have
fought a good fight, I have finished my course, I have
kept the faith" (2 Tim. 4:7).

(Thomas S. Monson, "Now Is the Time," *Ensign*, Nov. 2001,
60–61.)

DECEMBER 30
Importance of the Family

Pray in your families unto the Father, always in my name, that your wives and your children may be blessed.

3 NE. 18:21

See also "The Family: A Proclamation to the World" (*Ensign,* Nov. 1995, 102).

We are a church which bears testimony of the importance of the family—the father, the mother, the children—and of the fact that we are all children of God our Eternal Father. Parents who bring children into the world have a responsibility to love those children, to nurture them and care for them, to teach them those values which would bless their lives so that they will grow to become good citizens.

(Gordon B. Hinckley, *Teachings of Gordon B. Hinckley* [Salt Lake City: Deseret Book, 1997], 208.)

DECEMBER 31
Testimony of the Prophet

And now, after the many testimonies which have been given of him, this is the testimony, last of all, which we give of him: That he lives!

D&C 76:22

See also Luke 3:22; 3 Ne.11:7; JS–H 1:17.

I know that God our Eternal Father lives. He is the great God of the universe. He is the Father of our spirits with whom we may speak in prayer. I know that Jesus Christ is His Only Begotten Son, the Redeemer of the world, who gave His life that we might have eternal life and who rules and reigns with His Father. I know that They are individual beings, separate and distinct one from another and yet alike in form and substance and purpose. I know that it is the work of the Almighty "to bring to pass the immortality and eternal life of man" (Moses 1:39). I know that Joseph Smith was a prophet, the great Prophet of this dispensation through whom these truths have come. I know that this Church is the work of God, presided over and directed by Jesus Christ, whose holy name it bears.

(Gordon B. Hinckley, "We Look to Christ," *Ensign*, May 2002, 91.)

Index of Themes

About the Authors

ED J. PINEGAR

Brother Pinegar is a retired dentist and a long-time teacher of early-morning seminary and religion classes at Brigham Young University. He teaches at the Senior MTC and has served as a mission president in England and at the Missionary Training Center in Provo, Utah. He has been a bishop twice, and is a temple sealer and stake president.

Brother Pinegar and his wife Patricia are the parents of eight children, and reside in Orem, Utah.

RICHARD J. ALLEN

Richard J. Allen is a husband, father, teacher, writer, and organizational consultant. He has served on several stake high councils, in several stake presidencies, and as a bishop. Brother Allen has filled many teaching assignments in the Church, including full-time missionary, gospel doctrine teacher, and stake institute instructor. He has served as a faculty member at both Brigham Young University and The Johns Hopkins University. Richard has authored or co-authored many articles, manuals, and books, and loves to study the scriptures and Church history. He and his wife Carol Lynn have four children and live in Orem, Utah.